This book is a work of fiction. All characters, names, locations, and events portrayed in this book are fictional or used in an imaginary manner to entertain, and any resemblance to any real people, situations, or incidents is purely coincidental. This work is not intended as medical advice or relationship advice; please refer to an appropriate professional.

THE PERPETUAL CALENDAR OF INSPIRATION
Old Wisdom for a New World

Vera Nazarian

Cover Art:
"King David" by Andre Beauneveu, 1402.

Cover and Interior Design by Vera Nazarian

ISBN-13: 978-1-60762-083-9
ISBN-10: 1-60762-083-9

Trade Paperback Edition

October 15, 2010

Rev. 1.3.2023

A Publication of
Norilana Books
P. O. Box 209
Highgate Center, VT 05459-0209
www.norilana.com

Printed in the United States of America

The Perpetual Calendar of Inspiration

Old Wisdom for a New World

SPIRIT

an imprint of

Norilana Books

www.norilana.com

The Perpetual Calendar of Inspiration

Old Wisdom for a New World

366 Days of Insight from the Inspired.Us Blog

www.InspiredUs.com

Vera Nazarian

Welcome

This moment is the only moment during which you are alive.

Everything else is either a memory of the past or a dream of the future.

Use the moment well.

Daydream _____

_____
_____
_____
_____
_____
_____
_____
_____
_____
_____
_____
_____
_____
_____
_____
_____
_____

Wants and Needs

Life is a constant process of discrimination between wants and needs.

The low-carb muffin or the mocha latte? The new ultra-thin laptop or the latest phone and tech gadget? The rice or the uncontaminated water?

Don't feel guilty, don't feel envious, don't feel angry. Simply make your choice.

Because once the choice is behind you, then comes real gratification—the will to initiate change.

Thought _____

_____
_____
_____
_____
_____
_____
_____
_____
_____
_____
_____
_____

It's All in the Movement

Everyone's depressed, empty, useless—when stopping to consider one's life instead of simply going about the business of living it.

Really, think about it. Or better yet, no, don't—it'll only make you feel the "slow nothing" that is apathy, a harmful downer thing that lurks between the living moments like a bloated blah-troll. Sort of like when you put the movie on pause and go to use the bathroom—generally unrewarding, as experiences go.

I won't insult your intelligence and tell you to cheer up. Perky people grate on everyone's nerves (unless you are having your own perky moment, in which case, shoo!).

So what's the solution?

Simple. Keep looking for it! It's all in the movement. And yes, it exists.

Insight _____

_____

_____

_____

_____

_____

_____

Do . . .

Creativity is an excess of personal energy. What to do, oh what to do with it? The best use of this energy is when it's organized into meaningful constructs.

If you have too much energy and no outlet, just possibly you might need to create something, and soon.

Focus the energy into solid form of your choice. Use your hands, your mind, your ability to feel and interpret. That depressed, empty feeling will go away really fast. Sure, it's a temporary solution, but isn't time all we've got anyway?

Fill your time up with something that generates wonder.

Daydream _____

_____

_____

_____

_____

_____

_____

_____

_____

_____

_____

_____

Creating the Next Step

When making resolutions, we feel optimistic and energized. It seems as if we've focused our immediate future into a single powerful beam of clarity and shaped it, given it real, tangible form.

Indeed, it is exactly what happens.

In the creation of each new, concrete goal, we create the rest of our life.

Thought _____

_____

_____

_____

_____

_____

_____

_____

_____

_____

_____

_____

_____

_____

_____

_____

_____

_____

The Proper Way to Smile

The truest smile happens when the mouth remains immobile. It's in the way the eyes fill up with positive energy bursting to come out. And the muscles of the whole face take on a subtle "smile configuration."

There's really no way to fake that kind of smile. In any given moment, you either have it or you don't.

When the next genuine smile opportunity comes up, try smiling only with your eyes and keep that annoying mouth out of the picture.

Then, observe the impact.

Insight _____

_____

_____

_____

_____

_____

_____

_____

_____

_____

_____

Peace of Mind

The most precious treasure of all is peace of mind.

It can cure insomnia, lower your high blood pressure, improve circulation, help you achieve your ideal weight, allow you to cope with loss and daily hardships and financial hell, give you the confidence to be real, encourage you to love, and grace you with the ability to live—you know, all that good stuff.

How do you achieve piece of mind in this complex world?

The same way you would achieve anything else worthwhile.

Earn it.

So, get cracking.

Daydream _____

_____

_____

_____

_____

_____

_____

_____

_____

Expect the Unexpected

Some people love surprises, others hate it. Well, tough luck to the second group. Because that's what ordinary living gets you—one surprise after another, in a nonstop rollercoaster.

Unexpected things come in all sizes and all flavors, from tiny bad to huge wonderful, and vice versa.

The trick to dealing with the unexpected is to learn to maintain a personal balance that will act like a buffer for you against the thrown pies and baseballs and apples and bullets and gold coins that come your way in an unending stream.

You might not enjoy rollercoaster rides, but there's s good reason you are on this one, at this very moment.

And that reason is that somewhere somehow someone figured that you can take it.

Here's betting that someone was you.

Thought _____

_____

_____

_____

_____

Extrovert and Introvert

Laughter is an extrovert expression of the deepest joy and deepest sorrow.

Tears are an introvert expression of the same two.

Silence is one step beyond, into the realm of profound impact. It does not necessarily mean there is a lack of response or lack of understanding, but that your response is more intense and it cannot possibly be displayed... at least not yet.

Some things just cannot be expressed without undue complexity. And a good part of it is letting time process it, unravel the details like a tangled skein.

Complex reactions need to ripen like grapes on a vine.

So, take your time, as you would with fine wine, and never underestimate silence.

Insight _____

_____

_____

_____

_____

_____

_____

January 10

The Sin of Time

One sin seldom mentioned is that of killing time.

Daydream

The Function of Life

What is the meaning of life? So goes the eternal, popular, unanswered question.

Well just possibly it's the wrong question.

Everything and everyone in the world seems to have one or more function, an ability to perform or carry out a task or action. A function is a property of an object or an entity. It is like a jigsaw puzzle piece that through its specific shape is capable of filling an empty place in a greater whole—whether filling it with a material presence or action or effect or influence or movement. And, many entities and objects can fill more than one empty place along more than one dimension, and serve as multi-dimensional puzzle pieces.

A human being is a jigsaw puzzle piece for an almost infinite range of dimensions. We can do and be so many things and fill so many roles—lover, parent, enemy, confidant, foil, savior, cheerleader, deceiver, teacher, friend. The list stretches to infinity.

And one of our most complex and fulfilling roles is that of being alive, living.

Thus, the act of living is a function of us—the marvelous function of life.

No need to dwell on meaning. Simply let us perform this function to the best of our abilities.

Thought _____

_____
_____
_____
_____
_____
_____
_____
_____
_____
_____
_____
_____
_____
_____
_____
_____
_____
_____
_____

" When in the chronicle of wasted time
I see description of the fairest wights,
And beauty making beautiful old rhyme
In praise of ladies dead and lovely knights." Shakespeare.

Chasing Love

Don't look for love. That's like your dog chasing the beam of a laser pointer.

Exactly like that.

Think about it. Really, really think about it.

Insight _____

_____

_____

_____

_____

_____

_____

_____

_____

_____

_____

_____

_____

_____

_____

_____

_____

_____

_____

_____

Paradox

Paradox is the result of employing two different perspectives to observe or explain the same thing—the relative and the absolute.

It is like an optical illusion puzzle that constantly changes before your eyes while you decide how to *see* it.

There may be no right or wrong answer. But the choice to resolve the dissonance one way or another is always yours.

Daydream _____

_____
_____
_____
_____
_____
_____
_____
_____
_____
_____
_____
_____
_____
_____

The Flow of Wisdom

Once opened, like a dammed-up river, the flow of wisdom may not be quelled.

What the heck does that mean? Well, it's like they say, it'll open a can of worms.

Thing is, sometimes you want those worms all over the place. New idea worms can aerate the old, stuffy soil of your mind.

Thought _____

_____

_____

_____

_____

_____

_____

_____

_____

_____

_____

_____

_____

_____

Narrow Perspective

Losing perspective is being stuck in one single view of things and becoming distant from other views.

Imagine yourself stuck in a cable car or a ski lift somewhere halfway up a mountain. While the cable car is moving, you can see the whole world for miles around. Everything is beautiful, and you are in control. But when you are locked in place, suddenly the world seems to narrow in on you. Not only are you stuck, but you are also afraid and, quite frankly, unable to think clearly.

Fear and limitation are both the result of a limited perspective.

So, avoid both by always reaching out with your mind.

Insight _____

_____

_____

_____

_____

_____

_____

_____

_____

_____

_____

January 16

Fog and Desire

Desire is like fog on a bathroom mirror—its presence incites you to wipe the mirror and see yourself clearly again.

Daydream _____

_____

_____

_____

_____

_____

_____

_____

_____

_____

_____

_____

_____

_____

_____

_____

_____

_____

_____

_____

A True Immortal

Hope is the last thing that dies.

Maybe because hope is one of those dratted things that is truly, honestly, genuinely immortal.

Thought _____

_____

_____

_____

_____

_____

_____

_____

_____

_____

_____

_____

_____

_____

_____

_____

_____

_____

_____

_____

_____

_____

To Trust or Not?

Responsibility and Trust—these two are like Yin and Yang, together perfectly complete, and each one requiring the presence of the other.

The next time you mistrust someone, consider this—does that person feel responsible for you in any way? If the answer is yes, then go ahead and trust them. Very likely, they are looking out for your best interest.

Insight _____

_____
_____
_____
_____
_____
_____
_____
_____
_____
_____
_____
_____
_____
_____
_____

Life's Legumes

When trouble or misfortune hits, it is time to collect the pieces of your life together, like a bowl of spilled mixed grain, peas, and beans, and make some bread.

Or savory soup. Or some glue. Or some sand paintings. You've got imagination, you know. So, go wild, already.

And forget that spiel about the lemonade. Life never gives you lemons. That would be too easy.

Daydream _____

_____
_____
_____
_____
_____
_____
_____
_____
_____
_____
_____
_____
_____
_____
_____
_____

The Scientific Method of Forgiveness

To forgive is not to forget, but to re-examine in light of universal truth.

Okay, so some people do not believe in universal truth or any other absolutes or constants (well, possibly with the exception of the speed of light, or Planck's Constant, or Faraday's Constant, or Newton's Constant, or Avogadro's Constant.... okay, a number of scientific-community-approved constants).

So, then, how about this—instead of absolute, universal, perfect truth, imagine a truth that is just relatively larger in its scope that any individual person's.

Now, multiply it by the number of possible persons, sentient entities and perspectives in the universe.

And there you have it, a finite truth, and yet about as "absolute" as it can get under the circumstances and with our limited *homo sapiens* brains to quantify and grasp it.

So, in the light of that Very Large Truth, to forgive often involves seeing the other side from another rather stereophonic perspective—a whole bunch of perspectives, in fact—and most of all, seeing from the perspective of the actual person who has wronged you.

In doing this, you re-examine the event and the action itself from all possible sides. No panel of judges can do it, only you and your suddenly "expanded" imaginary perspective.

And in light of such observations, you just might possibly come to understand why the person did what they've done to you, and why, and how, and all the myriad life decisions and reasons and cause-and-effect chains that made it all happen.

And after such close and complex scrutiny, there is a very good chance that you will be able to forgive.

Of course, even that's not a guarantee of forgiveness, but a possibility.

But it's better than nothing.

Thought _____

_____
_____
_____
_____
_____
_____
_____
_____
_____
_____
_____
_____

LIBER

GENERATI

ONISIHU

XPIFILIIDAUIDFILII

ABRAHAM

Religious Interlude

When you come out of your Churches, O people, remember that God is present just as much in the open fields of morning, the wind, the mountains and the sky, the expanse of the sea, the radiant sun, in the sad eyes of the old dog on the roadside, and in the gaze of your mother upon you when she thought you were too young to see her love.

For those of us who do not look for religious interludes— simply go outside and take a deep, invigorating breath of air.

With or without faith, oxygen is always a good thing.

Insight _____

True Love

The truest love is always one-sided. It only matters that you love, not whether the object of your love responds to you.

Expect nothing in return.

Daydream _____

_____
_____
_____
_____
_____
_____
_____
_____
_____
_____
_____
_____
_____
_____
_____
_____
_____
_____

Method Acting

Method acting is a great tool for becoming.

In method acting, an actor immerses himself or herself into the role to the point of living 24/7 as that person, and never stepping out of character.

You and I don't need to be Laurence Olivier or Katherine Hepburn, but we can certainly try the method acting experiment to change ourselves by trying on another personality, and pretending to be what we are not... yet.

There is nothing stopping us—think about it. A game of pretend is one of those things we've enjoyed and excelled at since our childhood.

Thought _____

_____

_____

_____

_____

_____

_____

_____

_____

_____

_____

_____

Giving It All or Nothing

There's nothing like a real-life problem to take your mind off wallowing in your own self.

The sudden adrenaline rush, the sense of purpose, the focusing of energies to overcome the obstacle, and all your mental faculties sharpened and working hard to deal with the problem.

And the irony is, now is when you wish most that life was back to the boring, empty state and you can get back to that existential navel gazing.

Well, there's got to be some middle ground. It does not have to be all laze-and-sleep or fight-or-flee.

Part of the solution is setting up a series of real-life goals—both short-term and long-term—and not getting sidetracked.

So, how are your goals shaping up?

Insight _____

_____

_____

_____

_____

_____

Why Persist?

Persistence is an amazing thing.

It can be motivated by so many things, or even combinations of things inside you—pride, competitiveness, desperation, urgency, duty, passion, need, love, hate, self-confidence, desire, curiosity, stubbornness, courage, expediency, money, status, patriotism, loyalty, intensity, job description, boredom.... The list does not end.

However, persistence is impossible when the road ahead of you is obscured.

So, clear out that confusing debris and futile garbage and disappointing junk that is getting in the way of your goals, and you will suddenly find it is much easier to persist at your task indefinitely—for as long as it takes.

Daydream _____

_____
_____
_____
_____
_____
_____
_____
_____

Rulebook of the Universe

Life is but detail, the flow of data.

Conclusions based on this data are to be derived and organized into the Rulebook of the Universe.

The coolest thing is, the Rulebook is an ongoing, joint project, and we are all freelance contributors.

And, as such, one of these days we are bound to get paid.

Thought _____

The Passing On of Wisdom

Wisdom is restating the obvious and commonplace in a novel way, so that it makes sudden, pertinent sense.

Why do you think there are so many words out there? So many synonyms for the same thing? So many human languages?

It's because we all learn wisdom for ourselves, and in our own words.

And then we go on to teach others.

Insight _____

_____
_____
_____
_____
_____
_____
_____
_____
_____
_____
_____
_____
_____

Giving of Yourself

They say, "Give of yourself."

Who are they? Well, most everyone, it seems. This notion has become ingrained in many of our human societies—a mixture of religious, moral, ethical, humanistic, and humanitarian sentiment.

And what does it mean, to give of yourself? Besides, why should you?

Maybe, just possibly, we are all made of the same thing. No matter how "good" or "bad," worthy or unworthy, it is the same living matter, the same building blocks, the same energy.

So, when we give of ourselves, we simply add a little bit of this common "self" to the other person who might be in need of a little self-boost.

How do we do this? By communicating.

The neat trick is, no matter how many of our bits and pieces we dole out, we still end up complete and whole. We lose nothing.

Makes it very easy to be generous.

Daydream _____

_____

The Passionate and the Polite

Passion and courtesy are two polar opposite traits that serve to balance each other into a full-blooded whole.

Without socialization, passion is a crude barbarian, and without passion, the elegant and polite are dead.

Allow both passion and courtesy into your life in equal measure, and be complete.

Thought _____

_____
_____
_____
_____
_____
_____
_____
_____
_____
_____
_____
_____
_____
_____
_____
_____

Circle

The Circle, the Spiral, and the Pendulum, all point to the cyclic nature of the universe, things returning on themselves.

There is no proof of course, only patterns. They seem to indicate eternal, repetitive movement within the confines of the universal rules, the boundary.

If life is a great circle, then why not hold hands with the one who is closest to you and partake in a circle dance?

Insight

Lavender Crescent

When hope is fleeting, stop for a moment and visualize, in a sky of silver, the crescent of a lavender moon. Imagine it—delicate, slim, precise, like a paper-thin slice from a cabochon jewel.

It may not be very useful, but it is beautiful.

And sometimes, it is enough.

Daydream _____

Birds and Fish: Meditation Puzzle

Behold—the birds swim through the sparkling air, and the fish fly in the shimmering water—all in the depths of this sky ocean.

Where are we?

Thought _____

_____

_____

_____

_____

_____

_____

_____

_____

_____

_____

_____

_____

_____

_____

_____

_____

_____

_____

_____

_____

Soul Mates

Don't look for a soul mate.

Make one—out of the complex fabric of the human being already with you.

Instructions are never included. They vary with the strength of your ability to see, the measure of your selective blindness, the limits of your mercy, and the intensity of your desire.

Insight _____

_____

_____

_____

_____

_____

_____

_____

_____

_____

_____

_____

_____

_____

_____

Lessons of History

History does not repeat itself. It uses new terms each time—new shapes, locations, principal actors.

It is our obligation to discern the running motif and recognize the same play, because we are its playwrights.

History is—and has been always—under our control.

If anything, may this one thought always empower you.

Daydream _____

_____
_____
_____
_____
_____
_____
_____
_____
_____
_____
_____
_____
_____
_____
_____
_____

Sing

Sometimes, it is when you are happiest that you have the least to say, and when you are saddest that you have the most to say. At other times, things reverse.

To add another layer of difficulty, most of us constantly cross the line from one to the other. In the process, our words seem to betray us. We feel helpless, at the mercy of our mood-based verbal communication.

To regain control over your inner state... speak not a word.

Sing.

Thought _____

_____

_____

_____

_____

_____

_____

_____

_____

_____

Not Being Alone

To be alone with yourself is to be alone. To be in the company of others is to be alone together.

The only time you are not alone is when you forget yourself and reach out in love—the lines of *self* blur, and just for a wild, flickering moment you experience the miracle of *other*.

And now you know the secret.

Insight _____

_____
_____
_____
_____
_____
_____
_____
_____
_____
_____
_____
_____
_____
_____
_____

Joy

Joy is all around you.

Even in the deepest moments of personal hell, in sorrow and greatest tragedy, in death, futility, endless night—joy is all around you. Because joy is in the fabric of the world, in the fine nature of being.

Joy is a constant property of life. It is a permanent fixture that cannot be taken away.

Reach out with your hands—when you again find it in yourself—and feel joy.

Daydream _____

_____
_____
_____
_____
_____
_____
_____
_____
_____
_____
_____
_____

Your Desire

Desire creates the universe. Absence of desire negates the universe. Control of desire gives power over the universe.

So, what do you desire?

Are you sure?

Thought _____

_____

_____

_____

_____

_____

_____

_____

_____

_____

_____

_____

_____

_____

_____

_____

_____

_____

_____

_____

Dangerous Boredom

Boredom can kill.

Therefore, do something, before anyone gets hurt.

Insight _____

_____
_____
_____
_____
_____
_____
_____
_____
_____
_____
_____
_____
_____
_____
_____
_____
_____
_____
_____
_____
_____

Sage Somnolence

There are very few problems in this world that you and I cannot get a better handle on—and sometimes even resolve—after a simple, good night's sleep. Sleep is like the refresh button on your browser. It clears the screen cache of your mind.

Try to get to bed early tonight. Just this once, okay?

You'll thank me tomorrow.

Daydream _____

The Innocent and the Cynic

The naive innocent and the cynic are both equally distant from the truth—or, if you prefer not to use such an absolute term—from what is real.

One has seen too much of good (or maybe seen not enough of anything), the other too much of evil (or too much of the same thing). One has become biased and jaded with the passage of events and experience, the other has not yet learned that bias is possible and is still unfamiliar with ennui. One expects too much, and the other expects nothing.

Neither one is able to properly evaluate things.

I suppose, they should marry each other.

Or maybe not. That would be just too cruel.

They can simply go out on a first date.

Thought _____

_____

_____

_____

_____

_____

_____

Reality Entertainment?

Why do people watch reality shows? It's a strange abomination, and yet, addictive to so many of us.

The answer lies in a combination of expectations and control.

Many of us want to experience clean, refreshing, surprising, honest "reality." And yet we want the surprises to be only the good kind, want it to be predictable, and under our ultimate control—under anyone's control, as long as a hint of it is there.

What we really lust for is a series of plausible, free-form events that are plotted like a genre story, with the "genre" determined beforehand by the thematic focus of the reality show. This way we get the best of both worlds, the danger and raw energy of real living and the safety and pleasant entertainment values of controlled, meaningful art.

It is a comfortable illusion that straddles the edge between predestination and free will.

And in this complex world, it's the secret place we feel most comfortable being, for the moment.

Insight _____

_____

_____

Patience

Patience is not a virtue.

It is an achievement.

Daydream _____

Allowing In Responsibility

Face it.

It is a most wonderful ability to be able—at any time, and no matter what emotional condition your mind is in—to break out of the rut of your own personal existence, and face a responsibility that has caught up with you from the past.

In fact, why not do it *now?*

Take this moment and acknowledge that something needs to be done, and that you owe it to yourself and someone else to do it.

Relief will follow.

Thought _____

_____

_____

_____

_____

_____

_____

_____

_____

_____

_____

Love

Love—not dim and blind but so far-seeing that it can glimpse around corners, around bends and twists and illusion; instead of overlooking faults love sees *through* them to the secret inside.

— from "The Story of Love" by Vera Nazarian

Insight _____

Perspective on Pursuits

Science is an organized pursuit of triviality.

Art is a casual pursuit of significance.

Let's keep it in perspective.

Daydream _____

Personal Space

We all have something we consider personal space.

It is not just that immediate physical space of about three feet beyond which you don't feel comfortable allowing strangers to encroach, such as when someone stands talking too close to your face—you might call it the personal bubble—but the greater living space that you consider *home*.

It's your home turf, your haven, your refuge. The place that you occupy and organize according to your own needs, and the place you can lounge around in, relax, dream, be yourself, be safe.

It is also the place you clean, maintain to a certain level of personal comfort. And it is the place for which you are responsible and of which you are proud. (Now, if you don't bother to take care of your surroundings, or don't feel that you have such a place, it simply means that you still haven't discovered your true home, and you are still life's wanderer. But don't worry, your time of homecoming will come, as it inevitably does for all of us.)

So, what exactly is home, this personal space?

For some of us, it is just our room. For others, it is our whole house, even our whole property with its yard.

For others, it's the block on which they live, or maybe even the whole street.

Maybe, for yet some lucky others, it's the whole neighborhood, and even the whole community. And for yet others, it extends even beyond to city level, and then state and country level.

Then there are some of us who take it even further, and extend the sense of personal space to the whole continent, and just maybe, the whole surface of this living planet.

And why stop there? For some, personal space reaches out on the wings of thought into the solar system, and then our Milky Way Galaxy, and then our . . . universe.

Now, considering the fluid extent of all this personal space, how can you and I stand to *litter?*

Thought _____

_____

_____

_____

_____

_____

_____

_____

_____

_____

_____

_____

_____

_____

Real Endings

There is no such thing as a "bad ending"—it is just the low point of a sequence of events that hasn't yet played out to its completion.

And each sequence, like the proper swing of a pendulum, starts and stops on an upswing.

Try to remember this when you are at the lowest point.

That upswing is coming.

Insight _____

_____

_____

_____

_____

_____

_____

_____

_____

_____

_____

_____

_____

_____

_____

Clear Signals

The most difficult thing in the physical world is communicating precisely what you mean.

The language tools we have at our disposal—words, sounds, patterns, tone, gestures, etc.—are simply inadequate. For the most part, we communicate only a portion of our intent, like radios transmitting at an unreliable static-ridden frequency, or cell phones going in and out of range.

Assuming this, it makes good sense to be patient with the other person, and give them the benefit of the doubt when communication is problematic.

They may not be receiving and we may not be transmitting exactly what we all think.

Daydream _____

_____

_____

_____

_____

_____

_____

_____

_____

_____

Melting Away Fear

Laughter and love both dispel fear. Laughter is quicker, yet love is surer.

Notice how both of these sensations or emotions generate a state of inner warmth.

So, does this mean that fear is a cold, icy thing?

Thought _____

_____

_____

_____

_____

_____

_____

_____

_____

_____

_____

_____

_____

_____

_____

_____

_____

_____

Holy Foolish?

It takes a certain level of denseness, even stupidity, to be confident, relaxed, assured.

Those of us who are much more alert, cynical—and yes, cautious, wary, careful—we might sneer. And yet, we envy such people their seeming ease of bearing and the facility with which they carry themselves through life.

Often, it is their innocence and naïveté that gives them this peculiar advantage.

A lack of vision. Maybe, a lack of experience.

Because the moment you really stop and think, the moment you really break your living stride to take a close look around you with an intense, alert scrutiny, you come to realize that *everything* is dangerous. The next step you take, the next breath you inhale—all can derail you, and everything is a potential cause of harm.

It is a miracle indeed that anything persists—that we survive, that we can continue to live day to day.

Maybe being selectively blind is not such a bad thing. Enough with the details already—look at the big picture, the great, unified gestalt of the moving universe, the rhythm . . . Close your eyes partway and observe through narrow slits the changed, hazy world.

Pretty!

And suddenly it becomes an easy thing to walk the razor edge of a cliff many kilometers high.

There's a good reason some of us may be considered holy fools.

And there's a good reason that, when going to the beach, it pays to wear sunglasses and sunscreen.

Insight _____

_____

_____

_____

_____

_____

_____

_____

_____

_____

_____

_____

_____

_____

_____

_____

_____

_____

_____

_____

The Music of the World

When you see no reason to go on, no purpose, stop and listen to the music of the world.

Okay, did you listen?

Good—now tell me, what key is it in?

Daydream _____

_____

_____

_____

_____

_____

_____

_____

_____

_____

_____

_____

_____

_____

_____

_____

_____

_____

_____

_____

Immediate Goals

To have no immediate goals is worse than having no toilet paper once you've sat down on the seat.

It's like sitting down when the seat has been left raised.

As you can see, the solution is not merely advanced planning, but paying close attention to the exact situation and the nature of the moment at hand.

Also, a full-body-and-mind ability to maneuver fast can really come in handy.

Thought _____

_____

_____

_____

_____

_____

_____

_____

_____

_____

_____

_____

_____

Diamond or Rhinestone

How brightly shine the Diamond of Truth and the Rhinestone of Falsehood. . . .

On the other hand, it could all just be Cubic Zirconia, so just enjoy the pretty sparklies and don't worry about truth, underlying worth, or hidden flaws.

Sometimes surfaces are enough.

Insight _____

_____

_____

_____

_____

_____

_____

_____

_____

_____

_____

_____

_____

_____

Listen to This

Listening to others is not a fine art, but a learned craft.

You can hear what they say, but it does not mean you really hear what they are saying, but what you *think* they are saying.

How to know when you are only deluding yourself?

The answer is simple—practice listening. With enough practice, you will be on your way to knowing.

Practice, practice, practice.

Now, what was it that I just said?

Daydream _____

_____

_____

_____

_____

_____

_____

_____

_____

_____

_____

_____

Passion and Timing

Why is it that when there is no time, we burn to do so many things, and when we manage to have time, we seem to have no will to do them?

How can one get the timing right?

How can passion correspond with will? Isn't passion a form of will, that initial urge? What fiendish mystery of entropy is this?

Once thing is certain—procrastination is not completely at fault.

Some of it is our instinct, causing the hum of uncertainty, telling us that something else might be going on underneath the surface.

Thought _____

_____

_____

_____

_____

_____

_____

_____

_____

_____

Fit of Happiness

There is something that makes each one of us genuinely happy. And that something is a different thing for all.

Just a simple notion to keep in mind the next time we try to impose our own idea of happiness upon someone else.

Like a pair of nice pants in the wrong size, it may not fit.

Insight

Friendship is Rice Paper

Friendship is such a warm, clean, all-enduring, flexible, granite-hard, unbeatable, invulnerable, dependable, unconditional, mighty force.

And yet...

Friendship is such a delicate, precious, amazing, fragile, miraculous, impossible, one-of-a-kind, ethereal, vulnerable thing.

Please, don't ever break yours.

Daydream _____

_____

_____

_____

_____

_____

_____

_____

_____

_____

_____

_____

_____

_____

Fleeing Youth

The point at which you start feeling old comes suddenly upon you, out of the blue.

One moment you are young, and the next, you are on the downslope, it seems. And yet, it is not the true point from which you actually start becoming old.

It is merely the point at which you need to snap out of your rut, re-think your life and address your vital needs.

Life has just smacked you on the nose—wake up!

Thought _____

_____

_____

_____

_____

_____

_____

_____

_____

_____

_____

_____

Quantum Ghost

Today is an ephemeral ghost. . . .

A strange, amazing day that comes only once every four years. For the rest of the time, it does not "exist."

In mundane terms, it marks a "leap" in time, when the calendar is adjusted to make up for extra seconds accumulated over the preceding three years due to the rotation of the earth. A day of temporal tune up!

But this day holds another secret—it contains one of those truly rare moments of delightful transience and light uncertainty that only exist on the razor edge of things, along a buzzing plane of quantum probability. . . .

A day of unlocked potential.

Will you or won't you? Should you or shouldn't you?

Use this day to do something daring, extraordinary, and unlike yourself. Take a chance and shape a *different pattern* in your personal cloud of probability!

Insight _____

_____

_____

_____

_____

Escapees

Where has all the energy gone? The same place where passion ran off to, and where stamina escaped, where purpose retreated….

Oh, and it's also the exact same vacation spot where your hope is sneakily trying to slip away, even as we speak.

But hey—hold on to the dratted thing! Never, ever let it go!

Hope must always be at your side.

Daydream _____

_____
_____
_____
_____
_____
_____
_____
_____
_____
_____
_____
_____
_____
_____

Daily Dose of Garden

There's a recommended daily allowance of "garden" that we don't often hear about.

When was the last time you stepped inside a garden? Is there one in your back yard? In your neighborhood? Within reach?

No matter.

Go find a garden!

With all your being, with every pore, with every breath, you require it.

Thought _____

_____

_____

_____

_____

_____

_____

_____

_____

_____

_____

Wicked Things

Arguments are such wicked things.

They really are.

Arguments happen only at such times when we are unwilling to give each other a chance.

Most of the time arguments are caused by the need of all sides to be contrary, to perversely pretend they don't understand the exact, subtle—or not so subtle—meaning of the other person's words, when they really *do* understand if they would only choose to admit it. Why? In order to perpetuate the argument, of course.

And why, you might ask, would anyone want to do such a weird thing?

Well, often the act of arguing lets us vent a whole bunch of cooped up general irritation at the other person.

Thus, the need to argue is often a symptom of other unresolved issues.

Think about it the next time you argue—you are not really discussing the point but are beating against the wall that is the other person.

Maybe it's time to stop and try another way?

March 4

They say...

Heaven is delicious, restful peace.

Hell is intense, unresolved turbulence.

And earth? Earth, my friend, is a succession of both.

Which makes earth a kind of an entertaining place to be, if you're one of the living. Never an easy place to be, mind you. But then, whoever claimed that *easy* was fun?

Enjoy your stay.

Insight _____

Getting Caught Up In Relativity

Don't get caught up in relativity.

It is easy to start comparing yourself, your situation, your *everything*—to others. All it takes is an aware, thoughtful mind, and down you go into that pit of relativistic despair.

However, our ruminations and cross-comparisons can lead to false insights—a bottoming spiral of emotional dissatisfaction with ourselves—simply because the more we seem to know, realize, and compare, the more we forget that there are just as many other things we are not taking into account.

Indeed, all relative comparisons, all relativity is itself relative.

The only perfect assessment can come from a "perfect" viewpoint outside any and all relative points of the universe.

All you and I can do is periodically remind ourselves of this and try to keep our relativity-based self-criticism in check.

Daydream _____

_____

_____

_____

March 6

Before Conversation

Before beginning any conversation and throwing around variously-loaded terms . . .

Be armed with the perfect definition.

Thought _____

_____

_____

_____

_____

_____

_____

_____

_____

_____

_____

_____

_____

_____

_____

_____

_____

_____

_____

_____

Love's Filter

Love filters the truth masterfully through the delicate sieve of its recipient's individuality.

Truth in its raw state is often unsuitable for consumption.

If truth were bitter ground coffee, then love would be the filter through which hot, scalding water passes to mix with the concentrated grounds, and the end result is a palatable liquid drink that makes the world go round.

Drink up!

Insight _____

_____

_____

_____

_____

_____

_____

_____

_____

_____

_____

_____

_____

_____

Woman: Meditation Puzzle

A woman is human.

She is not better, wiser, stronger, more intelligent, more creative, or more responsible than a man.

Likewise, she is never less.

Equality is a given.

A woman is human.

Daydream _____

_____
_____
_____
_____
_____
_____
_____
_____
_____
_____
_____
_____
_____
_____
_____
_____

Money and Fire

Money is like fire.

It is only good when there's just the right amount of it, when it's properly contained, and under your control.

Thought _____

_____
_____
_____
_____
_____
_____
_____
_____
_____
_____
_____
_____
_____
_____
_____
_____
_____
_____
_____
_____
_____
_____

Excitement

Seems like one of the most underrated emotional states in our society is excitement.

When you are genuinely excited, people think you are either being silly or overly emotional. Excitement is considered to be a shallow emotional state—the stuff of rollercoaster rides and summer blockbuster action movies, of ephemeral, low-brow entertainment such as "tacky" genre fiction, and Las Vegas strip neon signs.

Common perception has it that nothing serious or profoundly significant is ever achieved as a result of simple, childish excitement and exuberance.

And yet, this is such a horrible fallacy.

Far from being an immature response, excitement is what drives the will to achieve. It is what elevates your emotional energy levels to the point which is necessary for creativity, and hence, for action.

Without excitement, no artist would paint, no writer would put down words on the page, no musician would play.

Without excitement, no scientist would pursue a track of thought, no athlete would struggle to compete, no business entrepreneur would succeed in their financial field.

Excitement carries us over the threshold of bland, mechanical activity into the realm of directed, energized movement with a purpose.

Never underestimate the power of excitement over your life.

Feel it right now!

Insight _____

_____

_____

_____

_____

_____

_____

_____

_____

_____

_____

_____

_____

_____

_____

_____

_____

_____

_____

_____

_____

Pleasant Surprises

Not everyone loves surprises, even when they are assumed to be pleasant.

That's because what seems like a good thing for one person is not always a good thing for another.

Surprise someone only with something they truly want. And if you are unsure, then simply don't.

Daydream _____

March 12

What is Truth?

"What is Truth?" Pontius Pilate asked, and many others asked, and continue to ask throughout history.

The answers came and continue to come, as varied as there are forms of conviction.

Here is one roundabout response.

If repression and frustration can lead to illness, then so does the repression of truth and the frustrated expression of truth. Thus, when truth is not allowed to come out freely, illness sets in.

Truth is simply that what is natural.

Thought _____

_____

_____

_____

_____

_____

_____

_____

_____

_____

_____

A Metaphor

On this material plane, each living being is like a street lantern lamp with a dirty lampshade.

The inside flame burns evenly and is of the same quality as all the rest—hence all of us are *equal* in the *absolute* sense, the essence, in the quality of our energy.

However, some of the lamps are "turned down" and, having less light in them, burn fainter, (the beings have a less defined individuality, are less in tune with the universal *All* which is the same as the Will to flame)—hence all of us are *unequal* in a *relative* sense, some of us being more aware (human beings), and others being less aware (animal beings), with small wills and small flames.

The lampshades of all are stained with the clutter of the material reality or the physical world.

As a result, it is difficult for the light of each lamp to shine through to the outside. It is also difficult to see what is on the other side of the lampshade that represents the external world (a great, thick, muddy ocean of fog), and hence to "feel" a connection with the other lantern lamps (other beings).

The lampshade is the physical body immersed in the ocean of the material world and the limiting host of senses that it comes with.

The dirt of the lampshade results from the cluttering bulk of life experience accumulated without a specific goal or purpose.

The dirtier the lampshade, the less connection each soul has to the rest of the universe—and this includes its sense of connection to other beings, its sense of dual presence in the material world and the metaphysical world, and the thin connection line to the wick of fuel or the flow of electricity that resides beyond the material plane and is the universal energy.

To remain "lit" each lantern lamp must tap into the universal Source of energy.

If the link is weak, depression and/or illness sets in.

If the link is strong, life persists.

This metaphor to me best illustrates the universe.

Insight _____
_____
_____
_____
_____
_____
_____
_____
_____
_____
_____

The Definition of Life

We all want different things.

Our desire determines our individuality. And, very possibly, it defines our life.

Can a robot or artificial intelligence (AI) desire, truly? Can a living being cease desiring completely?

Considering that a lowly virus exhibits autonomy and has the ability to reproduce, could it be that the possession of desire is the better definition of sophisticated life?

Think about what you desire.

And live.

Daydream _____

_____

_____

_____

_____

_____

_____

_____

_____

_____

Changing the World

Do you feel powerless to change the world?

After all, you and I are but a tiny cell in a huge cosmic body, an insignificant speck in a universe that stretches outward beyond all human scale. What can you or I do to affect the universe?

And yet...

All it takes is for one cell to become malignant with cancer, and the whole body is brought down and dies.

All it takes is for one cell to exhibit a beneficial mutation, and the whole body benefits and is eventually transformed into a new, better-equipped species.

Such are the two extremes illustrating the power of the individual.

And yet, it is easy to forget that the greatest long-term power exists in the cell that maintains the body in its current state and quietly carries out its innate function. It is neither cancerous, nor wonderfully different.

It simply *is*.

There are more than two ways of changing the world.

Thought _____

Balm of Silence

Silence is a state of mind.

It is a necessary resting point between each living moment.

Take the next moment to pause your complicated life and enjoy the brief sensation of relief.

Do this whenever you feel the need for peace.

Heal yourself with moments of silence.

Insight _____

Wizard

There are so many definitions.

The first one presents an image right out of a fairytale—an old, wise man in a long robe and pointy hat, wielding a wand with magical powers. Or, maybe a younger Harry Potter version.

Maybe the term "wizard" conjures the notion of someone who is particularly good at something—technology, science, computers, math, etc.

Or maybe yet, you think of stage magic shows or parlor tricks—smoke and mirrors.

Maybe you think of the occult.

Or racial prejudice.

Or maybe you are reminded of those wacky installation programs that load your software applications.

Halloween?

How about this definition, instead. . . . A wizard is one who has control of time—personal and universal. A wizard plans each second of existence, knows all the variables, and therefore can anticipate events.

Does that sound like you?

Concentration

Having trouble concentrating and being easily distracted is a symptom of so many things—issues, problems, actual real-time distractions, wrong starts, aimlessness, indecision, worry, fear, insecurity, pain.

Take the time to figure out which one (or more) applies to you.

Only then can you begin to work on a real solution.

Daydream _____

The Fourth Dimension

The fourth dimension is movement.

It generates space-time. It is the rate of progression.

The fourth dimension is the fourth ray of the compass rose, North, South, East, West.

Which one?

That is up to you to discover.

Insight _____

_____

_____

_____

_____

_____

_____

_____

_____

_____

_____

_____

_____

The Desert and the Ocean

The desert and the ocean are realms of desolation on the surface.

The desert is a place of bones, where the innards are turned out, to desiccate into dust.

The ocean is a place of skin, rich outer membranes hiding thick, juicy insides, laden with the soup of being.

Inside out and outside in. These are worlds of things that implode or explode, and the only catalyst that determines the direction of eco-movement is the balance of water.

Both worlds are deceptive, dangerous. Both, seething with hidden life.

The only veil that stands between perception of what is underneath the desolate surface is your courage.

Dare to breach the surface and sink.

Daydream _____
_____
_____
_____
_____
_____

Belief and Folly

Is it folly to believe in something that is intangible? After all, some of the greatest intangibles are Love, Hope, and Wonder.

Another is Deity.

The choice to be a fool is yours.

Thought _____

_____

_____

_____

_____

_____

_____

_____

_____

_____

_____

_____

_____

_____

_____

_____

Smart as a Whip

Being smart as a whip includes knowing when not to crack it.

Insight _____

_____

_____

_____

_____

_____

_____

_____

_____

_____

_____

_____

_____

_____

_____

_____

_____

_____

_____

Incantation

If you repeat things enough times, they somehow take root in reality. Proof of such is gossip, rumor, word of mouth, buzz, infamy, urban legend . . . story.

These are things that reside in the common consciousness—the plane of common imagination—shared images of our human race.

Unicorns and manticores, gryphons and dragons, mermaids and alien beings from the stars.

They are all somehow *real*.

Maybe that's the secret of being—bestow a label or a name by putting something into words, repeat in earnest, and witness your creation take on a life of its own.

Daydream _____

_____

_____

_____

_____

_____

_____

_____

_____

A Stroke of Inspiration

Inspiration comes in a flash.

Or does it?

Earthquakes, tornadoes, lighting strikes, hurricanes, volcano eruptions, floods, and other natural disasters, are all preceded by some kind of natural warning, sometimes giving us enough time to prepare for the ordeal ahead, and to escape to safety. At some level, there are always signs of things to come. Signs as minute as a held breath—a moment of silence before the storm.

We may not consider inspiration a disaster, but a rare valuable gift from who knows where. And yet, it too acts to throw us out of the ordinary moment of being, with a measure of violence.

Inspiration is dangerous.

Listen for its approach, smell it, taste it, feel the draft, see the change in the light.

Be prepared.

Thought _____

_____

_____
_____

Don't Tell

Philosophy is a religion.

Religion is a philosophy.

Everyone subscribes to at least one or the other, and hence, unwittingly, to both.

Don't tell them, or they might be upset.

Insight _____

_____

_____

_____

_____

_____

_____

_____

_____

_____

_____

_____

_____

_____

_____

_____

_____

Infectious Thing

Yawns are not the only infectious things out there besides germs.

Giggles can spread from person to person.

So can blushing.

But maybe the most powerful infectious thing is the act of speaking the truth.

Daydream _____

_____
_____
_____
_____
_____
_____
_____
_____
_____
_____
_____
_____
_____
_____

Be Not Alone and Afraid

What is fear? What is being alone?

Either a lack of trust or a lack of compromise.

The world is filled with so many wonderful *others* that none of us has the excuse to blame the lack of opportunity. If you cannot find what you need in your immediate vicinity, then move! Take the extra steps to expand your perspective and your panorama of choices.

And then . . .

Find the courage to trust someone and curb the pride that prevents you from flexibility.

Thought _____

_____

_____

_____

_____

_____

_____

_____

_____

_____

_____

Revolution

Revolutions happen on any scale.

Revolution of a nation is traumatic and bloody, like the amputation of a limb. As such, it should come as a last resort.

Revolution of a single cell is minute and delicate and wrought with uncertainty as to the end result.

Revolution of one human being is cause for celebration.

Insight _____

_____
_____
_____
_____
_____
_____
_____
_____
_____
_____
_____
_____
_____
_____

Without Relevance

Wisdom is profound only when understood.

Otherwise, it is but the crashing sound of the distant ocean surf—eternal and undeniable, but without relevance to you.

Daydream _____

_____

_____

_____

_____

_____

_____

_____

_____

_____

_____

_____

_____

_____

_____

_____

_____

_____

_____

_____

_____

_____

Serenity

Serenity is a blissful, healthy state of being and the result of inner balance.

It requires for so many things in our lives to be going "right" at the same time—aspirations, finances, relationships, health, basic stability of daily routine. Even a clean, attractive home environment and a comfortable bed may make a difference.

When something is out of whack—and for almost all of us it is usually the case—serenity is very difficult to achieve. You need to make a concerted effort to ignore that problematic thing before any kind of balance returns to you.

And when too many things are going wrong, attaining balance is almost a joke. Most of us are just holding on for dear life. Sounds familiar?

Now, it may be useful to tackle each problem one at a time—and so we do. But when too many new problems pop up, we still find ourselves sinking in a quagmire. Our lives amount to a mess and we feel like failures, since we cannot seem to get anywhere.

What to do? Is serenity such an unreachable thing?

Not at all, my friend.

It is all a matter of priorities.

Here is something to keep in mind. Our life goals are not set in stone. They can be changed at will. And herein lies the key.

Try setting serenity as your life's goal.

Then, do whatever it takes to work to achieve *it* alone and nothing else.

Once you're there—and you will be—then switch your set of goals back to your original, real track.

It is never too late.

Thought _____

_____

_____

_____

_____

_____

_____

_____

_____

_____

_____

_____

_____

_____

Experience and Fear

The more experience, the less fear.

At some midpoint, with the rising awareness of all possibilities the fear grows, but then again tapers off, as the knowledge of how to cope exceeds it.

Once you scale the fear mountain, from there on begins a marvelous trend. . . .

The less fear, the more experience.

Insight _____

_____

_____

_____

_____

_____

_____

_____

_____

_____

_____

_____

_____

_____

Sage Memory

A sage is a former fool who has become tired of himself.

A foolish sage is one who forgets this.

Remember, or come full circle.

Daydream _____

_____

_____

_____

_____

_____

_____

_____

_____

_____

_____

_____

_____

_____

_____

_____

_____

_____

_____

Destiny and Free Will

Believe it or not, the notions of free will and destiny are not mutually exclusive.

Predestination is the universal framework of limits (based on natural physical laws) placed upon us.

Free will is our infinite ability to make choices within that framework.

Because the universal scale is so great—and most of it constitutes an undiscovered frontier—our choices are only limited by our knowledge, our abilities, and our imagination.

To put it simply, the world is such a huge playground sandbox that we will never run out of sand or reach the faraway safety fence of destiny.

So go out there and play!

Thought

Beauty on the Surface

So often, in seeming injustice, beauty on the surface is the compensation for an empty heart, while the kind and deserving show a plain outward demeanor.

Only, there is nothing inequitable about it.

The universe is fair—if the barren souls were not granted *something* to make them sweet to others, then they would be forsaken.

Insight _____

_____

_____

_____

_____

_____

_____

_____

_____

_____

_____

_____

_____

_____

Over the Moon

The cow jumped over the moon because it *could*.

What's stopping you?

Daydream _____

Selfish Altruism

Selfishness is a simple, knee-jerk choice of the moment.

It is based on self-preservation, greed, fear, or plain, hungry need—for the most part, *id*-based impulse.

Whatever its basis, it is a short-term approach to things. Acting selfishly might benefit you now, but not so much in the long term.

Take an extra moment before making your self-based choice, to visualize ahead to the greater chain of events that will ultimately affect you and those who matter to you. Look days, months, years into the future.

Then, be truly selfish and choose altruism.

Thought _____

_____

_____

_____

_____

_____

_____

_____

_____

_____

_____

Mountains

Why is it that so many proverbs, aphorisms, and utterances of wisdom are made about mountains?

Mountains are symbolic of struggles, high or insurmountable goals, head-spinning freedom, rising above the crowd, conquering the self, aiming high, reaching the pinnacle, achieving greatness, breathing the air of success, gaining a sense of superiority, being high above the clouds, feeling ecstasy.

Mountains are said to be divine, natural, eternal, sacred. Mountains can even be euphemisms for female breasts.

Indeed, mountains in all their purple majesty are nothing short of metaphoric heaven.

And yet, here is another simple thing.

If you sit on a mountaintop too long, eventually you will have to come down.

Insight _____

_____

_____

_____

_____

_____

True to Yourself

Sometimes, being true to yourself means changing your mind.

Self changes, and you follow.

Daydream _____

_____
_____
_____
_____
_____
_____
_____
_____
_____
_____
_____
_____
_____
_____
_____
_____
_____
_____
_____
_____
_____
_____
_____

Natural Resource

Camels and dromedaries store water in their bodies. They are naturally suited to life in the desert.

Human beings store memories and dreams in the vast caverns of their minds. They are naturally suited to life in prison cells.

Don't allow the limitations of your surroundings influence your life will, limit your joy, and curb your drive.

You already carry the universe inside you.

Tap into it.

Thought _____

_____

_____

_____

_____

_____

_____

_____

_____

_____

_____

_____

_____

Lure of the Maze

The difficulty in dealing with a maze or labyrinth lies not so much in navigating the convolutions to find the exit but in *not entering* the damn thing in the first place.

Or, at least not yet again.

As a creature of free will, do not be tempted into futility.

Insight _____

Motion Sensors

We are all glorified motion sensors.

Some things only become visible to us when they undergo change.

We take for granted all the constant, fixed things, and eventually stop paying any attention to them. At the same time we observe and obsess over small, fast-moving, ephemeral things of little value.

The trick to rediscovering constants is to stop and focus on the greater panorama around us. While everything else flits abut, the important things remain in place.

Their stillness appears as reverse motion to our perspective, as relativity resets our motion sensors. It reboots us, allowing us once again to perceive.

And now that we do see, suddenly we realize that those still things are not so motionless after all. They are simply gliding with slow *individualistic* grace against the backdrop of the immense universe.

And it takes a more sensitive motion instrument to track this.

Daydream

The Secret of Intuition

What is intuition?

It is not a thing of esoteric forces; no magic is involved; nothing supernatural; no elusive mystery of extra senses. Neither is it a bag of parlor trick illusions or smoke and mirrors.

Intuition is nothing more than the ability to see smaller things and draw finer connections from the raw matter of the world around you.

Indeed, intuition is micro-logic—the kind of logic that is so fine-tuned in its pathways of semantic connections that it seems to escape the rest of your own much cruder macro-senses, and is thus mislabeled as irrelevant. Its basis is so refined that it appears invisible.

Logical subtlety is at the root of intuition—subtlety armed with finely honed senses that you already possess.

It is an acquired skill. As such, it is a force to be reckoned with.

For intuition is a razor-sharp surgical tool for gauging truth.

Thought _____

_____

April 12

Your Breath

The regular rhythm of your breath is the basis of everything you do. It is relentless and constant and reliable as clockwork.

And yet, if you stop to think about it for even one moment, you can "stumble" and lose the rhythm.

Such self-contemplation—an act of stepping outside yourself—can make you stumble in many other things.

Why not pretend for a moment that everything you do is like breathing?

Insight _____

_____
_____
_____
_____
_____
_____
_____
_____
_____
_____
_____
_____

Imagine

Imagine a world where lifestyle choices, belief, religion, moral values, and final judgment are all based on unconditional love and mercy.

Imagination is the greatest impetus.

Daydream _____

_____

_____

_____

_____

_____

_____

_____

_____

_____

_____

_____

_____

_____

_____

_____

_____

_____

_____

April 14

Open Mind

The wind blows with greater force through wide open spaces.

Open your mind wide and let the wind of thought range in freedom and clear out the stagnant detritus.

Thought _____

_____

_____

_____

_____

_____

_____

_____

_____

_____

_____

_____

_____

_____

_____

_____

_____

_____

Secret Weapon

Worry is the secret weapon unleashed upon us by the dark forces of the world that lurk in the shape of fear, uncertainty, confusion, and loss.

We, on the other hand, have our own secret weapon against these incorporeal fiends.

It is laughter.

Insight _____

_____

_____

_____

_____

_____

_____

_____

_____

_____

_____

_____

_____

_____

_____

_____

_____

The Five Senses

The five senses are the only things standing between each one of us and the rest of the universe.

It is possible that there is another sense—indeed, maybe an infinite number of other subtle senses—which we know nothing about.

But these precious five that we *do* know, we must guard and treasure and never lose track of, and hone their sharpness with all that is within us.

For, without our senses we are truly alone.

Daydream _____

_____

_____

_____

_____

_____

_____

_____

_____

_____

_____

_____

_____

Rain and Wisdom

Want to touch the upper atmosphere?

Next time it rains, leave a bucket outside and then come and dip your fingers in. There's a good chance that at least some of that water contains particles from on high.

Want to know the highest wisdom?

Step outside into a crowded street and listen. There's a good chance you will hear a line or two of something that expounds upon profound, absolute truth.

Thought _____

_____

_____

_____

_____

_____

_____

_____

_____

_____

_____

_____

The Search

Everyone's always searching for something.

It's either stuff we want, or need, or admire, or miss, or plain find fascinating. Sometimes, if we focus all our resources upon the object of the search, it becomes a violent obsession. But if we search the right way—light, airy, carefree—we indeed find wonder.

Searching is our human drive for fulfillment, completion, a life urge, a reaffirmation of the self.

In the searching lies joy.

Go look for something today!

Insight _____

_____

_____

_____

_____

_____

_____

_____

_____

_____

_____

_____

Pleasure: A Cup of Tea

Pick up a delicate, fine bone china teacup filled with the hot, freshly boiled brew of tea leaves—Darjeeling, or Assam, or your favorite black treasure.

First, lower your face, lips hovering just above the surface, allowing the subtle fragrant steam to wash over your skin, to bond with you and enter the pores. The warmth stands like a second skin.

Then, inhale the steam. . . .

Fill your lungs with warm, soothing, vapor-drenched air.

Exhale slowly, in complete peace.

Put your lips to the edge of the cup and linger. Feel its smoothness.

When the brew is no longer scalding but still hot enough to fill you with exultant, living fire, take the first sip. Draw in and taste the light, life-affirming liquid.

You are home.

Daydream _____

_____

_____

_____

Catalyst Dawn

Have you ever seen the dawn?

Not a dawn groggy with lack of sleep or hectic with mindless obligations, and you about to rush off on an early adventure or business, but full of deep silence and absolute clarity of perception?

A *dawning* which you truly observe, degree by degree.

It is the most amazing moment of birth.

And, more than anything, it can spur you to action.

Have a burning day.

Thought _____

_____

_____

_____

_____

_____

_____

_____

_____

_____

_____

The Great Flood

There is an empty spot inside all of us. Sometimes there is more than one.

The spot is like a tiny black hole. The nature of its vacuum is blacker than black, colder than cold, more hungry than a starving nation.

The spot-holes must all be filled, or you feel an empty heartache, ennui, a sense of waste, a lack of will to do anything with yourself, a loss of meaning, a general weakness of will.

If you do nothing about it, more "holes" develop, and with time you lose personal cohesiveness. Slowly, you diminish.

What to do?

Well, it's a bit of a trick to fill those empty spots.

It requires the Great Flood.

The Great Flood is an outpouring of life energy to generate a rising tide of selfhood.

What in the world does that mean?

Simple—it is a redirection of energy.

Energy rises from your center to the outside, like a fountain, and fills in all empty spots of vacuum as it fills all of you.

Every hole is plugged. Every need is met. All hunger appeased. The fabric that is "you" is repaired and strengthened.

The life energy rushes outward like a supernova, brimming past the borders of your "self."

How to get that energy? Where does it come from?

One might say, "it comes out of nothing." *It "comes" in answer to an effort you make to look for it.*

Indeed, the moment you begin to wonder, to think of it, it is there, just welling at the edges of your being—the life force.

So, go ahead. . . . Invoke it and use it to make the Great Flood.

Then, Fill Yourself.

Insight _____

_____

_____

_____

_____

_____

_____

_____

Antiphona. Post partū vir
go inuiolata permansisti:dei
genitrix intercede pro nobis.
Versi. Diffusa est gratia in la
bijs tuis. Respon. Propterea
benedixit te deus ineternum.
Pater noster. Et ne nos indu
cas intēptationē. Benedictio
Recibus et meritis bea
tissime gloriosissimeqz
matris semp virginis Marie:
omnium sanctorum et sancta
rum perducat nos dominus
noster iesus christus ad regna

Karma Smackdown

Karma has been a pop culture term for ages. But really, what the heck is it?

Karma is not an inviolate engine of cosmic punishment. Rather, it is a neutral sequence of acts, results, and consequences.

Receiving misfortune does not *necessarily* indicate that one has committed evil. But it is a *sufficient* indicator of something else.

And that something else can be *anything,* as long as it is a logical consequence of what has come before.

Consider: if you fall into a well, you are not a bad person who deserves to suffer—you are merely someone who took a wrong step. Or someone who had one drink too many. Or got a head rush due to poor circulation. Or forgot to wear your glasses. Or—

The reasons are plentiful, and all plausible. But the chain of cause and effect goes way, way back into the deepest, hoariest recesses of your personal past.

So never rule out retribution. But never expect it.

Daydream _____

_____

Freedom

Freedom is not a license to act but a license to exercise free choices in any given situation.

It is not a "free-for-all" but a "free-to-choose."

Always use tact, subtlety, mercy, compassion—in other words, your best judgment—to interpret your final choice wisely.

Because everyone else is making the same difficult choices as you are.

Freedom is a thing shared.

Thought _____

_____

_____

_____

_____

_____

_____

_____

_____

_____

_____

_____

Tears

Don't ever be ashamed to cry.

The outpouring of pent-up emotion is as necessary and inevitable as rainfall.

And it allows you to take the next breath and plant the next step.

Insight _____

_____
_____
_____
_____
_____
_____
_____
_____
_____
_____
_____
_____
_____
_____
_____
_____
_____
_____
_____

Following Dreams

There's a familiar saying we've all heard before—follow your dreams.

It is absolute nonsense.

If you follow a dream, you will be following it always, like the receding horizon, like a will-o'-the-wisp. Under no circumstances should you follow your dreams, for dreams are only shadows.

Instead, consider *what* it is that you dream about, and come up with a practical, goal-driven plan of action that will get you—or anyone—there.

Then, follow your own step-by-step achievement instructions, as you would a recipe.

Even a child can do it.

Daydream _____

_____

_____

_____

_____

_____

_____

_____

_____

Security

The feeling of security is one of the most underrated and unexplored emotional states out there. It is the vanquisher of stress, the bringer of inner peace, the enhancer of joy, the means to appreciating the transient wonder of the moment.

Security, when it comes, is like a soft, warm glow, rising to envelop you from all directions, until you are bathed in the unconditional light of simply *being*.

And in case you disdain security and all that it entails, consider this—those who strive for security are not merely wise, prudent, selfish, timid, or seeking the simplicity of childhood and the safety of the familiar.

They are the ones who truly understand how to provide it to others.

Thought _____

_____

_____

_____

_____

_____

_____

_____

_____

_____

Use Your Relief

Relief is a great feeling.

It's the emotional and physical reward we receive from our bodies upon alleviation of pain, pressure, and struggle. A time to bask in the *lack* of the negative.

And yet, think about it—relief is really the *status quo*, a negation of the suffering, a *nothing* in itself. It is the way things *were* before the pressure and struggle began.

So, is it a step back? A regression?

Or is it an opportunity to regroup, start over, and move in a different direction?

Use your moment of relief well.

Insight _____

_____

_____

_____

_____

_____

_____

_____

_____

_____

First Nourishment of the Day

For many of us it is a quickly snatched hot cup of coffee or tea, and maybe a portable energy bar or a breakfast sandwich wrapped in foil and received from a fast food window.

As we consume it—liquid or solid, hot or lukewarm or cold—we pay it only a smidgeon of our attention. Maybe the heat briefly scalds the mouth as we rush to swallow, or the familiar flavor strikes the taste buds with "eggness," or "cerealness" or any number of other well-known things we consume all our lives.

The rest of our attention is on the world around us— whether it is the road as we hold the wheel, or the work on the computer screen in our office. And thus, we rush to swallow, to chew, to blandly fill ourselves.

The first nourishment of the day, the energy that will power and drive us, is taken in without awareness, or appreciation.

It is a pity. Because if we took the proper time to focus upon it, it would do us more tangible good.

Daydream _____

_____

_____

_____

_____

The Stories

The story of your life and mine is told through words, but it is experienced through the senses.

So, how is it that words "dissolve" in the transformational barrier of our imagination and come out on the other end as smells, tastes, images, sounds and touches? What kind of mind magic is it that transports us from the perception of dead symbols to a participation in a vibrant living reality?

Well, it is not magic, but your own ability to connect to the rest of the world.

Without the willingness on our part to reach out and connect to others, stories would not exist. We would have no desire to participate in experiencing them, and hence in creating them.

We would not *know* them.

And you would not be reading this sentence. Indeed, you would not be reading at all.

Terrifying, isn't it? Well, good thing you can imagine the scenario, because in the act of doing so you are negating it.

So relax, and read on. The stories are all safe and waiting for you.

Harsh Teacher

Why is it that things become painfully important only when we find them gone?

While the sun shines, we pay no attention. While we see color, hear music, feel the softness of cotton, taste the tang of a ripe apple, we ignore them and take them for granted.

While those we love are with us, alive, we don't consider the profundity of it.

Don't allow loss to be your harsh teacher.

Open your eyes and *look* around you now, and *see*.

Insight _____

_____

_____

_____

_____

_____

_____

_____

_____

_____

_____

_____

May Day!

In the old days, May 1st was considered the coming of spring, and celebrated as a new beginning.

At one point, it even became an official distress call, spoken three times to request help.

In more modern times, it evolved to become the international day of the working people.

Whether the first day of May is Beltane, Samhain, Walpurgis Night, Labor Day, International Workers Day, Lei Day, Loyalty Day, Roodmas, or a bank holiday; whether it involves a carnival, marching in parades, the crowning of the Queen of May and circle dancing round the Maypole, be sure to remember that this day is extraordinary!

What is your May Day like?

Daydream _____

_____

_____

_____

_____

_____

_____

_____

_____

Like Gossip

Sometimes I think that wisdoms slip from my mind like drool from the lips of an idiot. . . .

Where's all this stuff coming from? Is it any good? Any good in, you know, the wisdom sense? Who am I to spout this stuff anyway?

Well, here's the thing. You too can find yourself shedding wisdom like cat hair if you only allow yourself the liberty of introspection. Think about what you alone know that no one else does. That one neat, wonderful, profound insight. It is fully yours. No one else on this planet of about six billion people understands it like you do.

Now, see if you can share it with someone. Bestow it, a gift of yourself.

Wisdom is like gossip. Except it's the good kind.

Thought _____

_____

_____

_____

_____

_____

_____

_____

_____

The Pucker-Up Test

Take this test:

Shape your lips into a kiss-pout. Go ahead, do it right now, regardless of whether you are alone or in a public place. Hold the pose for five seconds.

How did that make you feel?

Playful? Daring? Silly? Sexy? Empowered? Cool? Hot? Brazen? Wanting to whistle?

Whatever your reaction, take your pick.

And now, analyze what you chose. Because the result reflects your personal vulnerability.

Insight

Act of Love

One who truly loves, takes responsibility for others, regardless of ability, cause, guilt, fault, or preference.

If you are not anyone's brother-keeper, then find someone closest to you who is in need and become one. You will not need to look far, since we all can use a helping heart— for a hand alone will not do—whether we admit it or not. So, go ahead, choose any one of us and then lighten our burden with subtlety.

See through us.

Daydream _____

_____

_____

_____

_____

_____

_____

_____

_____

_____

_____

_____

_____

_____

Faith

Faith is so overrated.

It is also only a small part of the equation.

What good does it do if you and I *believe* in something when we don't take advantage of the knowledge and understanding that this faith gives us in order to act for the greater good?

An example of misused faith, taken from the Judeo-Christian tradition—Satan has great faith and believes in God.

Maybe it is better to love than to believe.

Thought _____

_____

_____

_____

_____

_____

_____

_____

_____

_____

_____

_____

_____

Irritation, Yours or Theirs

Irritation means one of two things—you are unable to get through to the other person, or you are no longer willing to try.

Maybe you are tired of beating your head against the wall, or find your fount of emotional strength exhausted, or your words fail you. It is also possible that you already tried your eloquent best and the other person simply cannot or will not listen.

Recognize which it is, and then either renew your effort to communicate with better clarity or do what you can to get away from the source of irritation.

Don't waste another minute.

Because perpetuating anyone's state of irritation— including your own—is as bad as letting a faucet perpetually run water.

Insight _____

_____

_____

_____

_____

_____

_____

_____

Cycle of Joy and Pain

When there is only joy, you overload, and the emotion becomes meaningless.

When there is only pain, you become numb and once again, emotion recedes into meaninglessness.

When joy and pain randomly succeed each other in an unpredictable random progression, the result is true personal involvement—real life.

Daydream _____

_____

_____

_____

_____

_____

_____

_____

_____

_____

_____

_____

_____

_____

_____

_____

Personal Justice

You cannot be fair to others without first being fair to yourself.

Know that a well-honed sense of justice is a measure of personal experience, and all experience is a measure of self.

Know that the highest expression of justice is mercy.

Thus, as the supreme judge in your own court, you must have compassion for yourself.

Otherwise, cede your gavel.

Thought _____

_____
_____
_____
_____
_____
_____
_____
_____
_____
_____
_____
_____
_____

Easy Virtue

Virtue is, when you look at it very closely, that which is after all most expedient.

Often, we manage to not merely justify our questionable actions but cloak them in a "moral" veneer.

It's seductive and easy to pretend that we are in the right. And it is very easy to come up with a gazillion justifications and excuses and then proceed to do what we wanted to do in the first place.

But, for once, let's not.

The right thing—here and now—is the one true alternative.

And self-delusion is only a postponement of responsibility.

Insight _____

_____

_____

_____

_____

_____

_____

_____

_____

The Heaviest Weight

The heaviest weight settles upon you when it is time to start something important. It's as if gravity has doubled suddenly, and you find yourself unable to move from the spot. You are transfixed by a combination of laziness, fear, procrastination, and just plain entropy.

This is none other than the weight of doubt—the subtle, evil thing that's making you question the worthiness, value, implications, and meaning of the act before you.

You know on some rational level this sensation of weight is only an illusion. And yet you tarry. . . .

It is for this reason that there is only one solution.

Before there's time to take another breath, quickly . . . just do it.

Daydream _____

_____

_____

_____

_____

_____

_____

_____

_____

Connected

If you believe that everything in the universe is connected, that there is a unifying grand design, and that the world is a tapestry of intertwined elements of one organic whole, then you must concede that your right to life, death, and the pursuit of happiness is not always strictly your own.

Have mercy on the ones you love and the ones who love you.

Be flexible.

Do not lose track of your self . . . and yet, know when to *concede self* to others.

Thought _____

_____

_____

_____

_____

_____

_____

_____

_____

_____

_____

_____

It Matters

It might seem as though whatever you do in your life does not matter on the great, universal scale.

But in truth, you and I, we don't *live* on a universal scale— gods do.

And because we live and create on a small, relative, *human* scale, surrounded by things that are tiny and yet profound to us, they, the tiny things, *do* matter—to us.

As they should.

All we are expected to do is try to achieve the greatest thing to which we can aspire on our own, relatively tiny scale. We may exist in a fishbowl, but if we can imbue our small fishbowl with glory and wonder until it is full to the brim, then we have not lived in vain, since it takes an infinite number of fishbowls to build up the universe.

It is good indeed that all things are relative, because this way we can strive at the level of our own kind, not more, not less. It is only when we consider things beyond our fishbowl that we may be thrown off-kilter and begin to doubt ourselves and our purpose.

When such a thing happens, we must stop, take a deep breath, and again find our own *true* place, and ignore the grandness, the *infinity* of the universal scale all around us that may seem a mockery of our tiny selves. It is not—it only seems that way to us because we are looking in a manner in which we should *not* be.

And as we take the grounding breath and resume our pursuits, we return to live to the utmost on our own scale.

An ant is not expected to move a mountain; an ant has no concept of a mountain, and no need to consider a mountain as a whole. And yet, an ant, which does not intend to move a mountain—by moving tiny individual grains—does.

Insight _____

_____

_____

_____

_____

_____

_____

_____

_____

_____

_____

_____

_____

_____

_____

_____

_____

_____

_____

Inspiration Around You

Inspiration is always nearby, everywhere around you.

It is you who must become a conductive rod, receptive to its lightning.

Daydream _____

_____

_____

_____

_____

_____

_____

_____

_____

_____

_____

_____

_____

_____

_____

_____

_____

_____

_____

_____

_____

_____

_____

_____

Lost

A thought lost is worse than a heart lost.

A home lost is worse than innocence lost.

A soul lost is impossible—it has merely been misplaced or buried deep beneath the debris of experience, chaos, pain, and time.

When the rushing flood waters grow calm and still once more, you must wait and watch for the other's soul to re-emerge, floating gently to the mirror surface. . . .

Living and immortal.

Don't be surprised—your own soul called it forth, calling like to like.

It's the secret reason why souls never die.

Thought _____

_____
_____
_____
_____
_____
_____
_____
_____

Movement of Light

A sparkle of tiny, iridescent elements upon crisp, fallen snow, illuminated by streetlamps. The pristine, spherical glitter of raindrops. The fierce undulation of liquid fire upon a sunlit ocean. The curves of shadow and brightness upon human skin. A homogeneous white glow of gathering mist. The sharp-to-soft fadeout and sudden contrast of pallor and depth in the petals of a rose.

All beauty comes down to a simple movement of light.

Insight _____

_____

_____

_____

_____

_____

_____

_____

_____

_____

_____

_____

_____

_____

_____

_____

Pieces of Imagination

Imagination is nothing more than the raw matter of all life experience mixed up into separate elements in your mind.

Some people have trouble mixing up the pieces in meaningful new ways. Those are said to lack imagination. Why? Complacence or cowardice? More likely it is ordinary distraction—a preoccupation with the concrete, pre-assembled world already before them.

Others rejoice in the opportunity to create purple elephants with golden hair, and flying cities, the ability to time travel, and talking porcupines with doctoral degrees.

Imagination is the mind's joyful sandbox, a spread-out game board.

Go, play!

Daydream _____

_____

_____

_____

_____

_____

_____

_____

_____

The Power of Blank Slates

Have you ever wondered why meditative techniques such as Zen and other "blank slate" inducers work to focus the mind?

Very simple—when you focus on nothing, the only thing you have is what's already *with* you—inside you, bothering you, burdening you, irritating and hurting you.

The blank slate tempts it forth, according to the laws of the physical world. It has been observed that matter tends to fill up and occupy empty space, and there is a perpetual resistance to vacuum.

So, the internal thought-matter comes out, slithers out, crawls out, to fill the vacuum of the blank slate imposed like a drainage catheter upon your busy mind, to fill the surface consciousness.

Use it to its full capacity.

Thought _____
_____
_____
_____
_____
_____
_____
_____

The View

Life's a room with a view.

It is always your choice to look or not to look outside the window at the world of possibilities.

Just don't complain of boredom when you don't. And remember that sometimes, glasses and telescopes are necessary.

Insight _____

_____

_____

_____

_____

_____

_____

_____

_____

_____

_____

_____

_____

_____

_____

_____

_____

_____

Epoch Epic

Every epoch needs an epic—a grand story of heroic deeds and larger-than-life individuals of the time. Epics are the only reliable and immortal time markers for the chronology of the human world.

When you find yourself looking back so far and finding nothing, and then relying on the ancients for a great story of their time—and yours—it is time to create a new epic for this age, for the here and now.

If you understand the importance of this, then proceed. Else your age will remain a blank, unmarked spot in the future chronology. . . .

As though it did not exist.

Inexcusable! Something must be done about it, by someone.

Maybe, you?

Daydream _____

_____

_____

_____

_____

_____

_____

Relinquish Reciprocity

Here is a tough call:

Give up all hopes of acknowledgment of your good deeds, your affections, your aspirations, your opinions, and ultimately your love.

Give up all expectations.

And now, assuming that you are surrounded by such an extremely indifferent universal vacuum, proceed to live your live filled with the fierce joy of knowing that you can still do all these things, still burn with the fire of the self, and that the reactions of others—or lack of such—matter less than the light breath of wind upon a great flaming furnace.

Remain aflame, because you must.

And because the above scenario is false.

Thought _____

_____
_____
_____
_____
_____
_____
_____

Death and Life

Life is vision.

Death is the blinking of an eye.

Insight _____

_____
_____
_____
_____
_____
_____
_____
_____
_____
_____
_____
_____
_____
_____
_____
_____
_____
_____
_____
_____
_____
_____
_____
_____

Elusive Treasure

A sense of wonder is such an elusive treasure. With the passing of time its perception seems to require more and more props and a greater intricacy of effects.

I look on with a fond yearning to the past when all it required was a dance of shadows against a wall for me to see epic tales.

Daydream _____

Equality

Equality is seeing oneself in the other person. Now, *what* you see is another matter.

It depends entirely on what you see in *yourself*.

Thought _____

_____

_____

_____

_____

_____

_____

_____

_____

_____

_____

_____

_____

_____

_____

_____

_____

_____

_____

_____

_____

_____

Change and Hope

Hope exists as long as change exists.

Insight _____

_____
_____
_____
_____
_____
_____
_____
_____
_____
_____
_____
_____
_____
_____
_____
_____
_____
_____
_____
_____
_____
_____
_____

Evolving Love

With years, my need for love has changed.

I no longer yearn for the lover but for the saint. I am not drawn to beauty, but to kindness. I desire not sensuality but warmth.

My passion has become a passion for wisdom.

Daydream _____

_____

_____

_____

_____

_____

_____

_____

_____

_____

_____

_____

_____

_____

_____

_____

_____

_____

_____

_____

The One You Love: Meditation Puzzle

Think of the one you love.

If, upon first consideration, you don't have such a person, you are not thinking hard enough, or you are unsure of the definition of love.

Think of the one you love.

Thought _____

_____

_____

_____

_____

_____

_____

_____

_____

_____

_____

_____

_____

_____

_____

_____

_____

_____

Belief and Elements

Why is it that we either fully believe in things that are flawed—such as sets of religious dogmas—or we believe in nothing at all?

We speak of elements of truth.

Let us assume for a moment that truth is indeed a natural element from the periodic table—it can be found in minute or large quantities in various substances.

If so, then let us look for—and expect to find—elements of truth in *all* things instead of expecting solid chunks of pure unadulterated truth in specific things.

Insight _____

_____

_____

_____

_____

_____

_____

_____

_____

_____

_____

_____

_____

Thought Fishing

Thoughts are slippery fish in a cold, shallow stream.

If you are intent on capturing a worthwhile one, you need to stand very still, focus very hard on *somewhere* outside yourself, and then simply ignore it until it gets so close that it tickles your ankles.

Then, pounce.

Daydream _____

_____

_____

_____

_____

_____

_____

_____

_____

_____

_____

_____

_____

_____

_____

_____

_____

Losing the Fire

They say that as we age, we lose the fire.

It is not so.

The fire is always there. Its nature is always the same, whether it flickers or burns raging and steady.

It is the source of *fuel* that becomes unreliable.

Thought _____

_____

_____

_____

_____

_____

_____

_____

_____

_____

_____

_____

_____

_____

_____

_____

_____

The Bill Rider of Evil

Pure evil hardly ever shows itself; it would be far too easy to see it and eradicate it.

Instead, evil attaches itself to good and tags along, like a bad bill rider attached to an otherwise benevolent law. Messy entanglement is evil's primary method of action.

So, the moral is: always read the fine print.

Insight _____

_____

_____

_____

_____

_____

_____

_____

_____

_____

_____

_____

_____

_____

_____

_____

_____

Storyteller's Secret

I'll tell you a secret.

Old storytellers never die.

They disappear into their own story.

Daydream _____

_____

_____

_____

_____

_____

_____

_____

_____

_____

_____

_____

_____

_____

_____

_____

_____

_____

_____

_____

_____

_____

Passion, Compassion, and the Unthinkable

Passion is human.

Compassion is divine.

Apathy is unthinkable. Okay, well, maybe it's all right if your name is Bessie, and there's a whole pasture filled with yummy grass. . . .

Thought _____

_____
_____
_____
_____
_____
_____
_____
_____
_____
_____
_____
_____
_____
_____
_____
_____
_____
_____

Two Voices

You know how we sort of have these two voices in our heads?

No, this is not about "crazy" people hearing things. And it's not about the devil or angel on our shoulder, the aftereffects of intoxication or sleep deprivation, or even dissociative identity disorder—no, this is all quite ordinary stuff.

One voice is what some people refer to as the voice of conscience or reason. And the second voice is the one that we mostly associate with the self, the so-called real *you* that is living in the here and now, and suffering or enjoying the moment.

So what happens is, we end up having these dialogues in out heads, pretty much unconsciously. But we hear the two voices become distinct only during particularly important decision points in our daily lives—the moments when we have to choose one thing or another, one way or another.

The "higher" voice of reason is usually making running commentary when we are unsure about what to do, when we are torn, lost, confused, hurting. It keeps is from jumping off a cliff or eloping to Vegas with the cute bartender. In the process of this mental dialogue and weighing of options, we justify our behavior or decisions to ourselves.

One of our voices—the immediate self—is usually emotional, impulsive, the one most in need of help or guidance. The other voice—which is also the self but a bit more detached, it seems—is consolatory, helpful, or critical, judgmental, supervisory. One is weak, the other strong. They constantly talk to each other, a sort of director's cut commentary track of our lives. But instead of being mere commentary, they are in fact making that movie on the fly.

Both of these voices are us—two equal sides of ourselves. Psychologists might assign various labels to this, our daily process of internal reasoning, while popular culture has other terms such as common sense, impulse, guts, chutzpah.

How about a new pair of terms, using metaphor?

Let's think, for a moment, of the self as a team of two techs on a mission. One tech is actually sitting back at the dispatch tower, watching the terrain. The other tech is down in the field, armed and equipped, and running through the jungle. The tech up in the dispatch many miles away—let's call her the Voice of the Absolute—sees the big picture and the progress of the tech who is on site. The tech in the jungle—let's call him the Voice of the Relative—is fully immersed in the moment, in the dangers of the jungle, the snakes and the vines and the bugs and the humid heat, and also the pleasures—the fresh, balmy air, the song of the forest.

It's rather easy for the jungle to overtake all senses, which is what happens to us in life as we live it. We are overwhelmed and forget the reality of the big picture beyond us when we can only see the mud at our feet as we wade through the swamp and the mosquitoes.

However, the person at the dispatch tower, an equal part of our team, can see all this too, except she also knows the reality of the sterile control tower and the equipment, the panoramic vista of land for many miles around, and she is also connected to a huge communication network. When she sees a snake hanging on a nearby branch, she can warn us without panic. But she also does not feel the heat or the painful rocks beneath our feet as we run—that's up to the guy on site to figure out and handle.

The Voice of the Absolute is our voice of *greater perspective*—reason, common sense, conscience, reality, and grounding—and she can give great mission support to the Voice of the Relative, the one who's in the thick of it all.

At any given moment of our lives we can choose to listen to that distant team member or not. If we do, we usually feel less lost and more in control. We can also avoid pratfalls and reduce the number of stupid mistakes we make if we're stuck only within the narrow, immediate perspective.

For best results, we're a team.

Next time we hear that dialogue in our head, let's not discount it. Instead, let us take the moment to listen to both voices—not only do things sound clearer in stereo, but it can be a great relief when we are feeling most alone.

And no, we're not "crazy," merely human.

Insight _____

Love Triangle

Love is made up of three unconditional properties in equal measure:

1. Acceptance

2. Understanding

3. Appreciation

Remove any one of the three and the triangle falls apart.

Which, by the way, is something highly inadvisable. Think about it—do you really want to live in a world of only two dimensions?

So, for the love of a triangle, please keep love whole.

Daydream _____

_____

_____

_____

_____

_____

_____

_____

_____

_____

The Child and the Adult

The child lives in *this* moment.

The adult lives in the contemplation of the past and future moments.

Key word: "lives"

Which of the two?

Thought _____

_____

_____

_____

_____

_____

_____

_____

_____

_____

_____

_____

_____

_____

_____

_____

_____

_____

_____

Why Not?

For as long as there's anyone to ask "Why?" the answer will always be, "Why not?"

Insight _____

_____

_____

_____

_____

_____

_____

_____

_____

_____

_____

_____

_____

_____

_____

_____

_____

_____

_____

_____

_____

_____

_____

_____

A Different Kind of Faith

Despite what you may have been told, faith does not constitute a belief in a Deity.

Faith is believing in your own hunches, your instinct, your true gut. Because no abstract, disconnected notion of Deity "out there" tells you more about truth and the way things are than that small voice inside of you that cries out to you, nags to you, whispers to you when you make any given choice—good, bad, or indifferent.

Trust and listen to it. It is never wrong. What is that voice anyway?

However, be careful that you don't get "radio interference" from all the other things stuck inside your head—hang-ups, biases, needs, and desires. The voice of true faith is clean and impartial.

And it is always right.

Daydream _____

_____

_____

_____

_____

_____

_____

_____

Spark of Insight

All the verbal pyrotechnics of poetry in the world do not measure up to one spark of insight.

Yet, insight framed by beauty flares from a spark to the brightest beacon of light.

Thought _____

_____

_____

_____

_____

_____

_____

_____

_____

_____

_____

_____

_____

_____

_____

_____

_____

_____

_____

_____

_____

_____

Fear and Frugality

Fear and frugality go hand in hand.

Notwithstanding one's means, poor or rich, it's those of us who are most afraid that hold on the tightest to their savings.

It's a risk to give, and an act of courage to thin down or even part with that external layer of material safety padding, by sharing it with others.

This holiday season, remember to make a personal sacrifice. Because you will almost certainly need help one day, and then you can hope with all your heart that there is someone out there brave enough to help you.

Be that brave someone now, for a friend in need.

Insight _____

People and Dry Skin

When dry cracked skin itches, it should not be scratched but soothed with moisturizing lotion.

The same goes for itchy, irritated people. Soothe them with the lotion of acceptance.

Otherwise, there will be a wound.

Daydream _____

_____

_____

_____

_____

_____

_____

_____

_____

_____

_____

_____

_____

_____

_____

_____

_____

_____

_____

The Difference Between
Love and Passion

Passion makes you vulnerable.

Love makes you vulnerable and hence, strong.

Thought _____

_____
_____
_____
_____
_____
_____
_____
_____
_____
_____
_____
_____
_____
_____
_____
_____
_____
_____
_____
_____
_____
_____

The Dark Secret

The dark secret is buried in pride, but it's not what you think. Pride is nothing more than a tantrum.

Sure, pride elevates you and sets you apart.

But pride also keeps you alone.

Do you like being universally alone, forever? Enjoy the sense of isolation from the rest of the universe? Bored to death yet, as your quite possibly brilliant mind turns into a sterile echo-chamber?

Well, you can stop it at any moment. It's completely up to you. And herein lies the dark secret.

Simply break your pride.

Grovel.

Grovel with all your heart before the universe.

It's only excruciating for the first few moments as the shell breaks... Then, you are filled with warmth and glorious light.

And you are once again as big and full as the universe.

Seriously, it's worth it.

Wisdom and Beauty

Why is wisdom so fair? Why is beauty so wise?

Because all else is temporary, while beauty and wisdom are the only real and constant aspects of truth that can be perceived by human means.

And I don't mean the kind of surface beauty that fades with age, or the sort of shallow wisdom that gets lost in platitudes.

True beauty grips your gut and squeezes your lungs, and makes you *see* with utmost clarity exactly *what* is before you.

True wisdom then steps in, to interpret, illuminate, and form a life-altering insight.

Insight _____

_____

_____

_____

_____

_____

_____

_____

_____

_____

_____

June Gloom

What a strange thing it is to wake up to a milk-white, overcast June morning! The sun is hidden by a thick cotton blanket of clouds, and the air is vapor-filled and hazy with a concentration of blooming scent.

The world is somnolent and cool, in a temporary reprieve from the normal heat and radiance.

But the sensation of illusion is strong. Because the sun can break through the clouds at any moment. . . .

What a soft, thoughtful time.

In this illusory gloom, like a night-blooming flower, let your imagination bloom in a riot of color.

Daydream _____

The Best Things

The best things—both material and intangible—in life are *earned*.

But occasionally certain unexpected good things come to us as a rare and precious gift, almost out of the blue.

How does that work?

To find out, give a small, heartfelt gift to someone, today.

Thought _____

_____

_____

_____

_____

_____

_____

_____

_____

_____

_____

_____

_____

_____

_____

_____

_____

Sun, Moon, and Starry Sky

Early summer evenings, when the first stars come out, the warm glow of sunset still stains the rim of the western sky.

Sometimes, the moon is also visible, a pale white slice, while the sun tarries.

Just think—all the celestial lights are present at the same time!

These are moments of wonder—*see* them and remember.

Insight _____

_____

_____

_____

_____

_____

_____

_____

_____

_____

_____

_____

_____

_____

_____

_____

Favorite Word

Here's a funny question:

What is your favorite word?

Think about it—maybe it's a word that makes you absolutely happy, or a word that sounds gloriously beautiful, or a word that evokes awe and wonder. Maybe you are reminded of a great time when you hear it, or maybe it represents your life's dream.

So, what is it? What is your favorite word of all words?

Thought about it yet?

Good.

And now, think *why*.

Daydream _____

_____

_____

_____

_____

_____

_____

_____

_____

Shoes and Purses and Pretty Rocks

Okay, why is it that women supposedly "love" shoes and purses and shiny, expensive trinkets? Seriously? Do *you*, if you're a woman? I mean, everyone loves a little bling, but do we *pretend* we love it more than we really do?

Also, is it the object itself that we are assumed to passionately crave, or what it represents? Status, prestige, beauty, youth, vigor, popularity, attractiveness, wealth. . . . A little of everything?

Did women always "love" these things, throughout history? Or were we taught to pretend to love and covet them in order to put us in a certain delineated frame of being, to contain us, and keep us "occupied" and easily *defined?*

And, as times change, will these specific material objects of desire give way to some others, such as fancy smart phones and gadgets?

It seems, the objects we covet represent society's current ideals.

What about our own true ideals? What do we *really* want?

Thought _____

_____

_____

Iced Tea: Meditation Puzzle

Imagine a delicious glass of summer iced tea.

Take a long, cool sip. Listen to the ice crackle and clink.

Is the glass part full or part empty?

Take another sip.

And now?

Insight _____

_____

_____

_____

_____

_____

_____

_____

_____

_____

_____

_____

_____

_____

_____

_____

_____

The Queen of Flowers

The rose is the queen of flowers.

She is an amazing blossom that embodies beauty, elegance, and love. And pride—don't forget the thorns. No other flower carries so much complexity, meaning, and impact through the ages.

What is this *something* about the regal rose that gives it such potent magic?

Look closely at the rose and answer for yourself.

Daydream _____

_____

_____

_____

_____

_____

_____

_____

_____

_____

_____

_____

_____

_____

_____

_____

June 20

In the Kingdom of Glass

In the kingdom of glass, everything is transparent, and there is no place to hide a dark heart.

Thought _____

_____

_____

_____

_____

_____

_____

_____

_____

_____

_____

_____

_____

_____

_____

_____

_____

_____

_____

_____

_____

_____

_____

_____

Secret Ignorance

It's a fact—*everyone* is ignorant in some way or another.

Ignorance is our deepest secret.

And it is one of the scariest things out there, because those of us who are *most* ignorant are also the ones who often don't know it or don't want to admit it.

Here is a quick test:

If you have *never* changed your mind about some fundamental tenet of your belief, if you have never *questioned* the basics, and if you have *no wish* to do so, then you are likely ignorant.

Before it is too late, go out there and find someone who, *in your opinion,* believes, assumes, or considers certain things very strongly and very differently from you, and just have a basic, honest conversation.

It will do *both* of you good.

Insight _____

_____

_____

_____

_____

_____

You or I?

Was it you or I who stumbled first?

It does not matter.

The one of us who finds the strength to get up first, must help the other.

Daydream _____

_____
_____
_____
_____
_____
_____
_____
_____
_____
_____
_____
_____
_____
_____
_____
_____
_____
_____
_____

Hold the Moon in Your Hand

Who says you cannot hold the moon in your hand?

Tonight, when the stars come out and the moon rises in the velvet sky, look outside your window, then raise your hand and position your fingers around the disk of light.

There you go. . . .

That was easy!

Thought _____

_____

_____

_____

_____

_____

_____

_____

_____

_____

_____

_____

_____

_____

_____

_____

_____

_____

Under the Lid

Secrets are such tantalizing things. They are like magnets. The moment you learn about the existence of one, you feel the overpowering need to uncover it.

Discovering the nature of secrets is one of the most powerful things that drive us.

But then, so many things drive us. Hunger, desire. A full bladder. A swarm of bees.

Keep in mind, some secrets, like packages of gourmet smelly cheese, may reveal more than you bargained for.

So before you lift the lid from that boiling kettle, be sure you have a thick potholder and towels, and a proper spoon to stir the unknown contents.

Insight _____
_____
_____
_____
_____
_____
_____
_____
_____
_____

Magical

Incidentally, the world *is* magical.

Magic is simply what's off our human scale . . . at the moment.

Daydream _____

The Road

The wide, open road is the single most hopeful thing in the world.

Look straight ahead and see it disappear into a point at the horizon.

That point is the future.

Seeing it, your lungs swell with joyful breath and buoyancy, and your heart feels a sweet, nostalgic tug forward.

The road is calling!

Sometimes, it is the road home.

Thought _____

_____

_____

_____

_____

_____

_____

_____

_____

_____

_____

_____

Act of Creation

One of the strangest things is the act of creation.

You are faced with a blank slate—a page, a canvas, a block of stone or wood, a silent musical instrument.

You then look inside yourself. You pull and tug and squeeze and fish around for slippery raw shapeless *things* that swim like fish made of cloud vapor and fill you with living clamor. You latch onto something. And you bring it forth out of your head like Zeus giving birth to Athena.

And as it comes out, it takes shape and tangible form.

It drips on the canvas, and slides through your pen, it springs forth and resonates into the musical strings, and slips along the edge of the sculptor's tool onto the surface of the wood or marble.

You have given it cohesion. You have brought forth something ordered and beautiful out of nothing.

You have glimpsed the divine.

Insight _____

_____

_____

_____

_____

Pleasure: The Wind

Close your eyes and turn your face into the wind.

Feel it sweep along your skin in an invisible ocean of exultation.

Suddenly, you *know* you are *alive*.

Daydream _____

Museum Awe

Some people think that museums are boring places filled with old things that no one cares about.

Tell them this:

The next time you enter a museum, walk quietly with stilled breath and sacred awe.

A museum is a holy shrine to the achievements of the human race.

It is in fact the most mind-blowing place to be, because it contains the only human-made things that are truly immortal.

Thought _____

_____
_____
_____
_____
_____
_____
_____
_____
_____
_____
_____
_____

Wise Marriage

Wisdom is nothing more than the marriage of intelligence and compassion.

And, as with all good unions, it takes much experience and time to reach its widest potential.

Have you introduced your intellect to your compassion yet? Be careful; lately, intellect has taken to eating in front of the TV, and compassion has taken in too many cats.

Insight _____

_____

_____

_____

_____

_____

_____

_____

_____

_____

_____

_____

_____

_____

_____

_____

Authorization

Respect the young and chastise your elders.

It's about time the world was set aright.

Daydream _____

_____
_____
_____
_____
_____
_____
_____
_____
_____
_____
_____
_____
_____
_____
_____
_____
_____
_____
_____
_____
_____
_____
_____

Message in a Klein Bottle

An infinitely self-replicating yet unending pattern suggests *something* about the flow of our lives.

Truth is inside-out.

Thought _____

_____

_____

_____

_____

_____

_____

_____

_____

_____

_____

_____

_____

_____

_____

_____

_____

_____

_____

_____

_____

_____

Main Course

Some people prefer eating dessert to the main course.

These people have never been really hungry.

Insight _____

_____

_____

_____

_____

_____

_____

_____

_____

_____

_____

_____

_____

_____

_____

_____

_____

_____

_____

_____

_____

_____

Patriotism

Patriotism is a thing difficult to put into words. It is neither precisely an emotion nor an opinion, nor a mandate, but a *state of mind*—a reflection of our own personal sense of worth, and respect for our roots. Love of country plays a part, but it's not merely love. Neither is it pride, although pride too is one of the ingredients.

Patriotism is a commitment to what is best inside us all. And it's a recognition of that wondrous common essence in our greater surroundings—our school, team, city, state, our immediate society—often ultimately delineated by our ethnic roots and borders . . . but not always.

Indeed, these border lines are so fluid. . . . And we do not pay allegiance as much as we *resonate* with a shared spirit.

We all feel an undeniable bond with the land where we were born. And yet, if we leave it for another, we grow to feel a similar bond, often of a more complex nature. Both are forms of patriotism—the first, involuntary, by birth, the second by choice.

Neither is less worthy than the other.

But one is earned.

Daydream

Holding Hands

Sometimes, reaching out and taking someone's hand is the beginning of a journey.

At other times, it is allowing another to take yours.

Thought _____

_____

_____

_____

_____

_____

_____

_____

_____

_____

_____

_____

_____

_____

_____

_____

_____

_____

_____

_____

_____

Far Seeing

Sunlight shimmers upon the waters like broken shards of a mirror.

Squint and look out across the ocean at the horizon.

You are seeing the future and the past, rolled into one.

Somewhere, thousands of years ago, another stood in your place, and looked and saw the same horizon.

Insight _____

_____

_____

_____

_____

_____

_____

_____

_____

_____

_____

_____

_____

_____

_____

_____

_____

Not So Random

Luck is not as random as you think.

Before that lottery ticket won the jackpot, someone had to buy it.

Daydream _____

_____

_____

_____

_____

_____

_____

_____

_____

_____

_____

_____

_____

_____

_____

_____

_____

_____

_____

_____

_____

_____

_____

Super Us

Ever been a one-person marching band? These days many of us are.

The last several years of financial, emotional and motivational turmoil have been incredibly challenging and tough in so many ways, which of course makes it very difficult to be creative. And at such a time, being creative is the one thing we *have* to be.

Almost requires a person to be superhuman to do it all.

You know what? Many of us *are*. What we do every day in order to pursue our dreams and at the same time hang in there and keep a roof over our heads and food in our bellies, is *amazing*. At one time or another, most of us are fulltime laborers, professionals, homemakers, nurturers, teachers, healers, inventors, providers, creators of artistic beauty, urban jungle warriors, saviors of the universe and everything else—all crammed into one person.

This really *is* the age of the super being. No wonder media supernatural heroes are so blazing-hot right now.

The world requires it.

Thought _____

_____

_____

Writer Ghost

Here's a strange fact. Writers, for the most part—especially writers of fiction—are doomed to be ever on the fringes of recognition, unknown, struggling, invisible.

It is not a myth. Most of us stay "starving" if we don't have some other job to pay the bills.

But, don't despair.

You and I may be a writer ghost (as opposed to a ghost writer—even those people seem to get more out of their careers than we do!). But the things we have to say are as corporeal and powerful as anything on the bestseller list.

Sometimes more.

So, keep on speaking to the clean vista of blank journal pages and the word processor screen.

Eventually your ghost words will haunt someone.

Insight _____

_____

_____

_____

_____

_____

The Saffron Shift

Science uses the Red Shift to measure deep cosmic distances. But how to measure deep historic time? How about—the Saffron Shift.

If history itself had a color, it is . . . like wood or bark, or living forest floor.

Assigning hues to time periods, the sum total of history is saffron-brown—but the chromatic arc starts from blinding white (prehistory) to sun-yellow (Ancient Greece), then deepening to pale wood tones (Dark Ages) and finally exploding like an infinite chord into a full brown palette that includes mahoganies, siennas (Middle Ages), oak, sandalwood (the Renaissance), cherry, maple (Age of Reason), and near-black old woods (Industrial Revolution) for which there may not be names.

As time approaches our own, the wood-brown palette fades to a weird glassy colorlessness, goes black-and-white for a brief span as you think of photographs of your grandparents, and then again fades until we get a clear medium that is the color of the world.

And the present moment is perfectly transparent.

It's only as you start looking into the future, that the colors start returning. The glass is turning silvery with a murky haze, and there is blue somewhere in the distance. . . .

Tease

Dangling a carrot in front of a donkey—or anyone else, for that matter—is not nice, and not fair, unless you eventually plan to give it up to them.

Thought _____

_____

_____

_____

_____

_____

_____

_____

_____

_____

_____

_____

_____

_____

_____

_____

_____

_____

_____

_____

_____

Strange Dreams

Strange dreams are better than no dreams at all.

Insight _____

_____
_____
_____
_____
_____
_____
_____
_____
_____
_____
_____
_____
_____
_____
_____
_____
_____
_____
_____
_____
_____
_____
_____

A Mirror: Meditation Puzzle

Who am I? I am you.

Look closely.

Daydream _____

Your True Name

Most of us have nicknames—annoying, endearing, embarrassing.

But what about your true name?

It is not necessarily your given name. But it is the one to which you are most *eager* to respond, when called.

Ever wonder why?

Your true name has the secret power to *call you.*

Thought _____

_____

_____

_____

_____

_____

_____

_____

_____

_____

_____

_____

_____

_____

_____

_____

Vegetable Secret

No one hates vegetables.

Instead, everyone hates to eat boringly prepared, bland, sterile, flavorless, washed-out, unseasoned food.

The vegetables are crying out to you:

"Spice me up! Pour interesting sauce over me! Mate me with compatible flavors! Put me in worthy recipes! Treat me as a worthy main course, not an afterthought side dish! Oh, and enough with that dull, horrid steaming, already!"

Listen to the vegetables.

Then, prepare to be amazed.

Insight

Tough Times

When tough times come, it is particularly important to offset them with much gentle softness.

Be a pillow.

Daydream

Siblings

It's a commonly expressed and rather nice, romantic notion that we are all "sisters" and "brothers."

Let's be real. Fact is, we might be better served to accept that we are all *siblings*.

Siblings fight, pull each other's hair, steal stuff, and accuse each other indiscriminately.

But siblings also know the undeniable fact that they are the same blood, share the same origins, and are family.

Even when they hate each other.

And that tends to put all things in perspective.

Thought _____

_____

_____

_____

_____

_____

_____

_____

_____

_____

_____

A Boomerang

A boomerang returns back to the person who throws it.

But first, while moving in a circle, it hits its target.

So does gossip.

Insight _____

_____

_____

_____

_____

_____

_____

_____

_____

_____

_____

_____

_____

_____

_____

_____

_____

_____

_____

_____

_____

Mobile Riches

It's easier for a rich man to ride that camel through the eye of a needle directly into the Kingdom of Heaven, than for some of us to give up our cell phone.

Daydream _____

Progression

Sunrise paints the sky with pinks and the sunset with peaches.

Cool to warm.

So is the progression from childhood to old age.

Thought _____

_____
_____
_____
_____
_____
_____
_____
_____
_____
_____
_____
_____
_____
_____
_____
_____
_____
_____
_____

Alphabet

Each letter of the alphabet is a steadfast, loyal soldier in a great army of words, sentences, paragraphs, and stories.

One letter falls, and the entire language falters.

Insight _____

_____

_____

_____

_____

_____

_____

_____

_____

_____

_____

_____

_____

_____

_____

_____

_____

_____

_____

_____

_____

_____

Afraid of the Dark

Don't be afraid of the dark.

Shine!

Daydream _____

The Fern and the Cactus

The cactus thrives in the desert while the fern thrives in the wetland.

The fool will try to plant them in the same flowerbox.

The florist will sigh and add a wall divider and proper soil to both sides.

The grandparent will move the flowerbox halfway out of the sun.

The child will turn it around properly so that the fern is in the shade, and not the cactus.

The moral of the story?

Kids are smart.

Thought _____

_____

_____

_____

_____

_____

_____

_____

_____

_____

Well-Groomed

The next time you visit the cosmetics counter, browse those rows of powders and creams, and are overwhelmed with a million shades of lipstick, blush, foundation, and eyeliner—consider the cat.

All it needs to stay well-groomed is its own saliva.

Insight _____

The Point

Why does every road eventually narrow into a point at the horizon?

Because that's where the point lies.

Daydream _____

_____

_____

_____

_____

_____

_____

_____

_____

_____

_____

_____

_____

_____

_____

_____

_____

_____

_____

_____

_____

_____

_____

_____

The Entrance

The still surface of a lake is a membrane separating the worlds of air and water.

It is a hair-thin sliver, as fine as a breath, the thickness of a blink, a single molecule of difference. . . .

Along this edge lies the entrance to Faerie.

Thought _____

Tornado and Earthquake

A tornado of thought is unleashed after each new insight.

This, in turn, results in an earthquake of assumptions.

These are natural disasters that reshape the spirit.

Insight _____

_____

_____

_____

_____

_____

_____

_____

_____

_____

_____

_____

_____

_____

_____

_____

_____

_____

_____

_____

_____

The Fastest Things

The only thing faster than the speed of thought is the speed of forgetfulness.

Good thing we have other people to help us remember.

Daydream _____

Your Story

Once upon a time, began the story of *you*.

Many perilous, wonderful, harrowing, brilliant, delightful, profound things happened.

And yet—the most exciting twists and best turns are yet to come. And it absolutely does not matter how old or young you are.

Like a bright carpet of wonders, enjoy the unrolling of your story.

Thought _____

_____

_____

_____

_____

_____

_____

_____

_____

_____

_____

_____

_____

_____

Friends

Friends are a strange, volatile, contradictory, yet sticky phenomenon. They are made, crafted, shaped, molded, created by focused effort and intent. And yet, true friendship, once recognized, in its essence, is effortless.

Best friends are formed by time.

Everyone is someone's friend, even when they think they are all alone.

If the friendship is not working, your heart will know. It's when you start being less than perfectly honest and perfectly earnest in your dealings. And it's when the things you do together no longer *feel right*.

However, sometimes it takes more effort to make it work after all.

Stick around long enough to become someone's best friend.

Insight _____

_____

_____

_____

_____

_____

_____

Reaching for Everything

When you reach for the stars, you are reaching for the farthest thing out there.

When you reach deep into yourself, it is the same thing, but in the opposite direction.

If you reach in both directions, you will have spanned the universe.

Daydream _____

Дѣвица, взявъ зеркало, вqду въ чашкѣ, восковыя свѣчи, и сѣно *Русская Святочная гаданіе на Курица* роняетъ пери, вбросавъ щепки, сѣно въ бутылкѣ, подъ вечеръ при
вала все это на полъ; туда пускаетъ и кури Сѣто ли куры Еваиеятъ, оттого осмилюсь, а если ли осудетъ кленовой верхъ, жоии
на поблюдетъ на зеркало и поглядитъ въ нее. правное, и во мое время пекли

Какова ти единой мой кушичи
Бывала ли пусты мои роба?
Вотъ выходу диженииа
Или прииимъ что была прошлой

В семъ городѣ Москвѣ 185? Марта 12 Кридоръ въ Варшо.

Певоть, въ Москвѣ летография Б Гунаиева

Your Throne

If you're confident enough, then any chair on which you sit down becomes a throne.

Thought _____

_____
_____
_____
_____
_____
_____
_____
_____
_____
_____
_____
_____
_____
_____
_____
_____
_____
_____
_____
_____
_____
_____

Out on a Limb

If you go out on a limb, know the way back to the trunk.

Say, what are you doing up in that tree anyway?

Insight _____

_____
_____
_____
_____
_____
_____
_____
_____
_____
_____
_____
_____
_____
_____
_____
_____
_____
_____
_____
_____
_____
_____

Watermelon Ocean

Watermelon should never be eaten by the slice, or with a polite fork in a fruit salad.

It is an elemental force of nature—an ocean of juices and sweet, crisp, windy freshness and super thirst-quenching, passionate abandon.

Dive into watermelon, and wallow in it. Stick your face in it, and pig out.

Consider it your surprise moment of sensual freedom.

Daydream _____

_____
_____
_____
_____
_____
_____
_____
_____
_____
_____
_____
_____
_____

The Bridge

Once upon a time, there were two countries, at war with each other. In order to make peace after many years of conflict, they decided to build a bridge across the ocean.

But because they never learned each other's language properly, they could never agree on the details, so the two halves of the bridge they started to build never met.

To this day, the bridge extends far into the ocean from both sides, and simply ends halfway, miles in the wrong direction from the meeting point.

And the two countries are still at war.

Thought _____

_____
_____
_____
_____
_____
_____
_____
_____
_____
_____
_____
_____

Inspiration

A church, a temple, a cathedral, is merely a building until it is consecrated.

A woman or man is merely human, until she or he is (or they are) inspired.

Insight _____

_____

_____

_____

_____

_____

_____

_____

_____

_____

_____

_____

_____

_____

_____

_____

_____

_____

_____

_____

_____

_____

The Fountain

Unlike a fountain that circulates the same water in an enclosed, perpetually recycling system, a human being circulates thoughts in an unlimited reservoir of self.

Don't limit yourself to being a mere fountain when you contain an ocean.

Daydream _____

_____
_____
_____
_____
_____
_____
_____
_____
_____
_____
_____
_____
_____
_____
_____
_____
_____
_____
_____

Fiction and the Intangible

Fiction is the fundamentalist interpretation of the imaginary realm, metaphors given solid flesh, and imagination fixed in the stone of material being. . . .

Fiction lets us touch what is otherwise out of reach.

Thought _____

_____

_____

_____

_____

_____

_____

_____

_____

_____

_____

_____

_____

_____

_____

_____

_____

_____

_____

_____

_____

The First Sign

The first sign of sanity is an open mind.

The first sign of "insanity" is rigid thinking.

The first sign is just that—a beginning, a first step.

Never forget that you always have the option to walk in another direction.

Insight _____

An Earworm

Earworms are songs that annoyingly stick in your mind, and refuse to go away. You hum them until someone tells you to stop. And then you hum again.

Usually these snippets of song have a pronounced melodic arc, and move in a circular manner, returning to the same note on which they began.

If you have something you'd like people to remember— opinions, facts—put them in the form of an earworm.

If you want these people to pay attention to your opinions and facts and *not* be put off and annoyed . . .

Then don't.

Daydream _____

_____
_____
_____
_____
_____
_____
_____
_____
_____
_____
_____
_____
_____

Fulfillment and Creativity

Consider this notion: fulfillment curbs creativity, while lack of fulfillment stimulates creativity and expression.

And yet . . .

The state of fulfillment is but an *instant,* while the rest of the time continuum is that of unfulfilled urge.

Wow, that's one mighty powerful end-game temptation carrot being dangled before us!

So how does creativity fit in this equation?

Creativity is a method and process. It is constructive and ongoing. And one of its most curious functions is to *prolong* and enrich this fundamental urge and desire, without quite achieving the end goal of fulfillment.

Creativity is what gives us control and enhances the precious instants of fulfillment when they do come upon us.

Thought _____

_____

_____

_____

_____

_____

Happiness: Meditation Puzzle

I am happy.

I have something to accomplish, create, and achieve.

I am happy.

Insight _____

_____
_____
_____
_____
_____
_____
_____
_____
_____
_____
_____
_____
_____
_____
_____
_____
_____
_____
_____
_____

Telling the Truth

Telling the truth is always the right thing to do. However, telling the whole truth *all at once* is not always the wisest.

Truth is a potent spice, a strong spirit, a bracing, concentrated tonic. And as any such, it is best to season to taste, and to consume in moderation.

Don't worry, you'll use up the whole bottle eventually.

Daydream _____

_____
_____
_____
_____
_____
_____
_____
_____
_____
_____
_____
_____
_____
_____
_____
_____
_____
_____

Dreamers

It is interesting that we call something good a "dream," but being called a "dreamer" is somewhat of a putdown.

Without dreamers, no dream would ever be given reality, and we would live in a very small and shallow world.

If you are a secret dreamer, it's your time to announce yourself.

Thought _____

_____
_____
_____
_____
_____
_____
_____
_____
_____
_____
_____
_____
_____
_____
_____

Creative Buffet

Creativity is not so much a boundless well, but an all-you-can-eat buffet of elements for your creative endeavor.

Eventually, you've eaten your fill, and it's time to digest and then make something.

But at some point, it will be time to return to the restaurant.

Insight _____

_____
_____
_____
_____
_____
_____
_____
_____
_____
_____
_____
_____
_____
_____
_____
_____
_____
_____

Saving Money

It's often a meaningless platitude to tell people to "save money" and "live on a budget," when the basic problem is, no matter how hard some of us work, we don't make enough to make ends meet.

No advice can help when you are subsisting instead of living, and all your life energy is put into drudgery.

Don't judge.

Don't give advice.

Give a helping hand.

Daydream _____

_____

_____

_____

_____

_____

_____

_____

_____

_____

_____

_____

_____

Maps

Maps are things of magic.

You look at the world flattened into two dimensions on paper, and yet imagine it in infinite layers, directions, and transparencies.

What is a map of a human being?

The palm of your hand.

Thought _____

_____
_____
_____
_____
_____
_____
_____
_____
_____
_____
_____
_____
_____
_____
_____
_____
_____

Playing

There's a difference between playing and playing games.

The former is an act of joy, the latter—an act.

Insight _____

_____

_____

_____

_____

_____

_____

_____

_____

_____

_____

_____

_____

_____

_____

_____

_____

_____

_____

_____

_____

_____

_____

_____

_____

Sense of Security

A sense of security is a precious state of mind—labor-intensive to achieve and precarious to sustain.

So many of us work hard for most of our lives just for a glimmer of it.

Security comes in so many flavors—personal, financial, emotional, spiritual, intellectual.

Never take your sense of security for granted.

Be a security guard for all.

Daydream _____

_____
_____
_____
_____
_____
_____
_____
_____
_____
_____
_____
_____
_____
_____

Mother

A mother is the most intimate and beloved being outside ourselves.

For your first years, she was your whole world.

For her last years, may you be hers.

Thought _____

_____

_____

_____

_____

_____

_____

_____

_____

_____

_____

_____

_____

_____

_____

_____

_____

_____

Home

One of the most difficult things in life is losing a home for which you've worked all your life.

There are no words.

The heart bleeds.

Then you pick up the objects that mean home to you. And you pack them up, and you uproot yourself and your loved ones.

And you go to plant your heart in a new spot of earth. Good thing the world is a big, wondrous place.

And every inch of it is home.

Insight _____

_____

_____

_____

_____

_____

_____

_____

_____

_____

_____

The Master of the Garden

The master of the garden is the one who waters it, trims the branches, plants the seeds, and pulls the weeds.

If you merely stroll through the garden, you are but an acolyte.

Daydream _____

_____

_____

_____

_____

_____

_____

_____

_____

_____

_____

_____

_____

_____

_____

_____

_____

_____

_____

_____

_____

_____

August 22

Good Book

Whenever you read a good book, somewhere in the world a door opens to allow in more light.

Thought _____

_____
_____
_____
_____
_____
_____
_____
_____
_____
_____
_____
_____
_____
_____
_____
_____
_____
_____
_____
_____
_____
_____

Your Beginning

What is the earliest thing you can remember? What is your first memory?

Think back as far as you can.

And now, share it with someone you love.

Insight _____

_____

_____

_____

_____

_____

_____

_____

_____

_____

_____

_____

_____

_____

_____

_____

_____

_____

_____

The World

"More often than you realize it, the world is shaped by two things—stories told and the memories they leave behind."
— from DREAMS OF THE COMPASS ROSE by Vera Nazarian

Daydream _____

Exception to the Rules

To every rule there is an exception—and an idiot ready to demonstrate it.

Don't be the one!

Thought _____

_____

_____

_____

_____

_____

_____

_____

_____

_____

_____

_____

_____

_____

_____

_____

_____

_____

_____

_____

_____

The Speaking Trees

Listen to the trees as they sway in the wind.

Their leaves are telling secrets. Their bark sings songs of olden days as it grows around the trunks. And their roots give names to all things.

Their language has been lost.

But not the gestures.

Insight _____

_____

_____

_____

_____

_____

_____

_____

_____

_____

_____

_____

_____

_____

_____

_____

Indirect

Never look directly at the sun.

Instead, look at the sunflower.

Daydream _____

August 28

Smooth Polished Rock

A wise person is like a smoothly polished rock: it takes time to become either.

Thought _____

_____

_____

_____

_____

_____

_____

_____

_____

_____

_____

_____

_____

_____

_____

_____

_____

_____

_____

_____

Strength

Strength is the willingness to try again, after you know you *can't*.

Insight _____

_____

_____

_____

_____

_____

_____

_____

_____

_____

_____

_____

_____

_____

_____

_____

_____

_____

_____

_____

_____

_____

_____

The Farmer's Market

At the farmer's market, everything is fresh, grown or crafted with pride. The produce beckons and the wares tempt.

Grow and craft your ideas and opinions to the same exacting standards before you take them to market.

Daydream _____

_____

_____

_____

_____

_____

_____

_____

_____

_____

_____

_____

_____

_____

_____

_____

_____

_____

_____

_____

Dramatic Exit

Late Summer is a rich matron in a cherry-red dress, laden with necklaces of carnelian, ruby, jade, amber, malachite, and agate, stepping out on the crimson carpet of Fall.

From her footfalls erupts maple fire.

Thought _____

_____

_____

_____

_____

_____

_____

_____

_____

_____

_____

_____

_____

_____

_____

_____

_____

_____

_____

_____

_____

_____

Back to School

Going back to school is exciting on the first day.

On the second, you get homework.

On the tenth, you finally remember why you're going to school in the first place.

And it's exciting.

Insight _____

_____

_____

_____

_____

_____

_____

_____

_____

_____

_____

_____

_____

_____

_____

_____

_____

_____

Abilities

A great ancient poet was blind.

A great classical composer was deaf.

Many of us are dumb.

What have we to show for it?

Daydream _____

A True Prophet

A true prophet comes to awaken each one of us *individually* to the truth of the world.

A preacher who leads *en masse* or demonstrates power, has ulterior motives.

Thought _____

_____

_____

_____

_____

_____

_____

_____

_____

_____

_____

_____

_____

_____

_____

_____

_____

_____

_____

_____

_____

September 4

Treasures

The greatest treasures cannot be stolen because they cannot be resold.

They can only be given away.

Insight

You Are Alive

For as long as you have the ability to make choices, you are *alive*.

Daydream _____

_____

_____

_____

_____

_____

_____

_____

_____

_____

_____

_____

_____

_____

_____

_____

_____

_____

_____

_____

_____

_____

_____

_____

September 6

Visiting Distant Places

Whenever you go on a trip to visit foreign lands or distant places, remember that they are all someone's home and backyard.

Thought _____

In the Plains

In the plains the grass grows tall, since there is no one to cut it.

There is no one to water it either.

Insight _____

_____

_____

_____

_____

_____

_____

_____

_____

_____

_____

_____

_____

_____

_____

_____

_____

_____

_____

_____

_____

_____

_____

Love Potion

Once upon a time, a young man obtained a magic love potion and gave it to the young woman he loved.

The next day she left him.

Don't worry about either one of them.

Daydream _____

_____
_____
_____
_____
_____
_____
_____
_____
_____
_____
_____
_____
_____
_____
_____
_____
_____
_____
_____

Locked Out

In times of misfortune and dire financial struggles, it is easy to think of yourself as someone suddenly locked out of your home. You are standing in the rain and freezing wind, getting cold, soaked, and weaker by the minute.

There's no doubt about it, you are screwed.

You can either wait around for someone to come and get your door open, you can try to find the key, or even get a new one made. You can go and knock on your neighbor's door. You can take a walk and hope a coffee shop is open—oh, wait, you don't have your wallet. . . .

Sometimes things get so bad, you cannot do any of that nonsense.

Time to break a window or a door, and just get inside.

Thought _____

_____
_____
_____
_____
_____
_____
_____
_____
_____

Coliseum of the Surreal

The poets huddle together in the corner like football players.

And the ball players are out before an audience, performing modern poetry in motion.

You sit watching, with your thumb ready to signal victory or defeat.

Insight _____

_____
_____
_____
_____
_____
_____
_____
_____
_____
_____
_____
_____
_____
_____
_____
_____
_____
_____
_____

Heroes

There are so many things that make a hero.

Heroes sacrifice themselves for others and for the greater good. Heroes quietly do what is right and perform their duty against all odds. Heroes fight for truth and uphold justice. Heroes are larger than life.

Heroes give themselves up as tools unto the benefit of others, surrender their life, their fate, their being, completely.

Heroes are all that's good and right with the world.

Heroes are also invisible until someone realizes who they are—which sometimes never happens at all.

Good thing it completely doesn't matter.

Daydream _____

September 12

Broken Vase

A fine glass vase goes from treasure to trash, the moment
it is broken.

Fortunately, something else happens to you and me.

Pick up your pieces.

Then, help me gather mine.

Thought _____

_____
_____
_____
_____
_____
_____
_____
_____
_____
_____
_____
_____
_____
_____
_____
_____
_____

Dark Righteousness

One of the worst, secret wrongdoings of our time is a propensity to *righteousness*. Armed with "facts" and irrefutable arguments, we accuse, condemn, and pronounce judgment on others.

Even if we are right, we are doing a disservice to all by being inflexible. By closing ourselves up to others' beliefs and opinions, we are closing doors of communication and windows of understanding—which swing in both directions.

For as long as we are "too correct" to listen, we are too limited to be fair.

Insight _____

_____
_____
_____
_____
_____
_____
_____
_____
_____
_____
_____
_____
_____

Renewal

Even if a tree sheds a hundred thousand leaves, it remains alive, from year to year.

What do we have that can be just as easily cast aside and renewed?

Our mindset.

Daydream _____

_____

_____

_____

_____

_____

_____

_____

_____

_____

_____

_____

_____

_____

_____

_____

_____

_____

Signs

Signs of all great things are written right before our eyes, in a near-invisible *code* of strangeness, wonder, and beauty. Sometimes, it's a shape, at other times, a color, or a sound, a single pure note. It is also a scent, or a brief, feather touch.

We look upon the world every day and see something simple, ordinary and commonplace.

But occasionally, something takes our breath away.

That's when we are given a glimmer of the true signs.

Today, watch closely.

Thought _____

_____

_____

_____

_____

_____

_____

_____

_____

_____

_____

_____

The City

In a haze of fog and smog the city shapes itself in the distance, angular skyscrapers marking the skyline with dreary, man-made geometry.

But with evening, golden lights appear in windows, winking into existence like fireflies, until the city is a jewel of infinite blinking eyes.

This is what takes place inside us at the moment of insight.

Insight _____

_____
_____
_____
_____
_____
_____
_____
_____
_____
_____
_____
_____
_____
_____

Pleasure: Raspberry

Raspberry is the flavor of utmost complexity.

All sensory depths are represented and contained in the sophisticated balance of taste layers—rich earthiness, ripe sweetness, biting tang, cool forest, and warm hearth.

Raspberry is loaded with history and potential, with delight and promise. Raspberry is a jewel and a flirt—and your one true, mature love of a lifetime whom you meet in the latter part of your journey. . . .

Consume a handful of raspberries today, and taste them truly for the first time.

Daydream _____

_____

_____

_____

_____

_____

_____

_____

_____

_____

_____

_____

_____

_____

September 18

As the Rain

Rain beats against the world outside in torrential streams of sky water.

It washes away everything.

May our forgiveness do the same.

Thought _____

_____

_____

_____

_____

_____

_____

_____

_____

_____

_____

_____

_____

_____

_____

_____

_____

_____

_____

The Windmill

The windmill is an ingenious yet simple invention that uses the natural force of wind to generate energy.

If the wind has so much untapped potential, imagine how much a human being has.

Bring out this immense potential with education and encouragement.

Don't let the wind steal it away for itself. Look how much it's taken already. . . .

Insight _____

_____

_____

_____

_____

_____

_____

_____

_____

_____

_____

_____

_____

_____

_____

_____

September 20

In the House

When you have many children and many animals living in your house, you might as well give up on keeping perfect order and strict housekeeping.

There is no *clean* in this house, only *love*.

Daydream _____

_____

_____

_____

_____

_____

_____

_____

_____

_____

_____

_____

_____

_____

_____

_____

_____

_____

_____

_____

_____

A Long Time Ago

A long time ago, people believed that the world is flat and the moon is made of green cheese.

Some still do, to this day.

The man on the moon is looking down and laughing.

Thought _____

_____
_____
_____
_____
_____
_____
_____
_____
_____
_____
_____
_____
_____
_____
_____
_____
_____
_____
_____
_____

Your Best Friend

Your best friend is sitting on your lap, purring, and at your feet, wagging his tail.

Curled in a soft ball, your best friend lies on the windowsill, or perches on top of the stuffed chair, to be near you.

When you come home, your best friend greets you at the door, dancing with joy, and watching you with impossible attention.

When you cry, your best friend gets up and comes to you unconditionally, so that you can put your hands on the warmth and rest against the beloved fur.

Don't ever forget.

Don't ever abandon them.

Insight _____

_____
_____
_____
_____
_____
_____
_____
_____
_____

Feat of Imagination

No feat of imagination can transform that jelly donut into
a slice of gourmet cheesecake.

No feat of imagination can transform that casual date into
the love of your life.

But sometimes, it's better than nothing.

That is, if you don't mind donuts.

Daydream _____

_____
_____
_____
_____
_____
_____
_____
_____
_____
_____
_____
_____
_____
_____
_____
_____
_____
_____

Training Day

When you start a new job, the first day is all introduction, orientation, and training.

But while you are soaking up their methods and ways, most curiously, they are learning from you.

Be an *interesting*, secret teacher. And hold on to that new job!

Thought _____

_____
_____
_____
_____
_____
_____
_____
_____
_____
_____
_____
_____
_____
_____
_____
_____
_____
_____

The Secret of Generosity

Generosity seems to be second nature with some people. They are never afraid to share or even give up their possibly last belongings, never worry about being repaid, and always respond immediately.

They know a secret many of us are unaware of, or choose to deny.

In this world, *nothing* belongs to us. Everything is borrowed. Everything can be taken or given away.

Only generosity is wholly ours.

Insight _____

_____

_____

_____

_____

_____

_____

_____

_____

_____

_____

_____

_____

_____

_____

Pleasure: An Old Bookshop

When you enter an old bookshop, you are assailed with a musty whisper-scent of antiquity and many minds.

This is a moment of truth. So much lies before you that you *don't* know. So many unread books, to be discovered.

There is intellectual vertigo. There is regret that you cannot read everything at once. And there is greed. Everything is coming together to press on you with giddy energy, as it is bubbling and rising. . . .

The world of past and present and future and *alternate* has been flattened and compressed between old paper pages.

All is stilled, holding its breath, waiting for you.

Daydream _____

_____
_____
_____
_____
_____
_____
_____
_____
_____
_____
_____
_____

The Hourglass

The sand in the hourglass runs from one compartment to the other, marking the passage of moments with something constant and tangible.

If you watch the flowing sand, you might see time itself riding the granules.

Contrary to popular opinion, time is not an old, white-haired man, but a laughing child.

And time sings.

Thought _____

_____

_____

_____

_____

_____

_____

_____

_____

_____

_____

_____

_____

_____

_____

_____

_____

Four Magic Words

"You have a point."

Without these words there can be no reconciliation in arguments, and no hope of peace.

Say these words because the opposite side always has *some* point you can find, if you are willing to listen.

Their point might even rest on faulty underlying arguments, or be irrelevant, or be an example of circular reasoning. But it can be used as a *starting point* for common understanding.

Be the first to say these four magic words the next time your argument is going nowhere, and watch the magic happen.

Insight _____

_____

_____

_____

_____

_____

_____

_____

_____

_____

The Pursuit of Luxury

Many people confuse the pursuit of happiness with the pursuit of luxury.

Luxury is a state of mind.

It is a general *sense* of having only the best things surrounding you. And since the best things mean different things to different people, after a certain level, luxury is an illusion hinging on perceptions of other people as much as yourself.

Strive for reasonably good things that make you happy, but don't push for the unobtainable best.

This way, you get to draw the luxury line for yourself, even when you live in a hovel.

Daydream _____

_____

_____

_____

_____

_____

_____

_____

_____

_____

Faced with a Mountain

If you are faced with a mountain, you have several options.

You can climb it and cross to the other side.

You can go around it.

You can dig under it.

You can fly over it.

You can blow it up.

You can ignore it and pretend it's not there.

You can turn around and go back the way you came.

Or you can stay on the mountain and make it your home.

Thought _____

_____
_____
_____
_____
_____
_____
_____
_____

Heart of Autumn

Autumn is the season of introspection. A cool exterior and a warm, orange middle, falling leaves and evenings before the glowing, exposed heart of fire.

Nature slows down to think.

Receive its burning heart as offering, be receptive, and allow the warmth inside.

Insight _____

_____

_____

_____

_____

_____

_____

_____

_____

_____

_____

_____

_____

_____

_____

_____

_____

_____

Apple Cinnamon Joy

When apple is wedded to cinnamon, the resulting aroma is the happiest smell in the world.

Something delightful is baking, and anticipation is rising like that pie crust, while exuberance fills the air with culinary music.

It's a glorious dance of scents and flavors at a harvest wedding.

Daydream _____

_____

_____

_____

_____

_____

_____

_____

_____

_____

_____

_____

_____

_____

_____

_____

_____

_____

Inspiring Individuals

How many individuals can you think of who are truly your inspiration?

How many of them are in your family? What about in your field of professional expertise? Your neighborhood or locality?

How many are celebrities? How many are historical personalities? Fictional characters?

Why aren't any of them *you?*

Enough excuses; inspire yourself!

Thought _____

_____

_____

_____

_____

_____

_____

_____

_____

_____

_____

_____

_____

October Moon

Something wonderful happens to the moon in October. First, it grows plump and yellow, transforming into a juicy peach, then into a bright orange pumpkin—great and fat and ripe like the last harvest.

The full moon floats in the cooling sky that has lost the last of its bright summer blue, and can only display the indigo and silver grays.

The season of depth has arrived.

Time to turn inward.

Insight _____

_____
_____
_____
_____
_____
_____
_____
_____
_____
_____
_____
_____
_____

Author's Secret

No book is ever truly finished—the author simply makes the conscious agonizing choice to stop fiddling with it . . .

. . . and then there's this thing called a deadline.

For that matter, no book is ever truly begun—the author stares at the blank sheet, starts drawing stick figures and monstrous ducks on the corners . . .

. . . and then there's this thing called a deadline.

Daydream _____

Fashionably Late

Being fashionably late is a strange phenomenon.

It is a reflection of artificial social graces and a measure of your dominant position in the group power hierarchy.

It is also an anachronism, subtly disrespectful to the host.

If you are visiting true friends, never be fashionably late.

Get there honestly, as soon as you can.

Thought _____

_____
_____
_____
_____
_____
_____
_____
_____
_____
_____
_____
_____
_____
_____
_____
_____

Dominoes

We are all dominoes, lined up closely in an endless circle.

But in the moment of falling we also prop each other up.

Insight _____

_____

_____

_____

_____

_____

_____

_____

_____

_____

_____

_____

_____

_____

_____

_____

_____

_____

_____

_____

_____

_____

_____

_____

Some Puzzles

Not every puzzle is intended to be solved.

Some are in place to test your limits.

Others are, in fact, not puzzles at all. . . .

Daydream _____

_____

_____

_____

_____

_____

_____

_____

_____

_____

_____

_____

_____

_____

_____

_____

_____

_____

_____

_____

Teacher

Don't waste your life looking for a wise teacher to help you to deal with things you don't know.

Instead, teach others the things that *you* know.

Thought _____

_____

_____

_____

_____

_____

_____

_____

_____

_____

_____

_____

_____

_____

_____

_____

_____

_____

_____

_____

_____

_____

_____

Autumn Sun

The sun in the autumn sky is the exact same sun as the one in the summer sky.

It's everything else that's different.

Insight _____

_____

_____

_____

_____

_____

_____

_____

_____

_____

_____

_____

_____

_____

_____

_____

_____

_____

_____

_____

_____

_____

Arch of Many Hues

After the rain stops on a bright day, there is often a shimmering wonder in the sky—an arch of many hues, that stands up like a bridge to *elsewhere*.

Inspiration is what takes you to the foot of that bridge.

The climb is up to you.

Daydream _____

_____

_____

_____

_____

_____

_____

_____

_____

_____

_____

_____

_____

_____

_____

_____

_____

_____

_____

Love at First Sight

Falling in love at first sight is no different than picking out the prefect dress.

It *can* happen.

But you still don't know for sure until you've taken it to the dressing room and tried it on in front of a mirror.

Thought _____

Honeymoon

Every year, the sun goes on a honeymoon to warmer climes—or is it that it brings the warmth with it, transforming the places it visits?

We, meanwhile, are left to bask in the residue of its loving glow.

It is just barely enough.

But love always returns the following year.

Insight _____

_____
_____
_____
_____
_____
_____
_____
_____
_____
_____
_____
_____
_____
_____
_____

The Divine Stereo

Each living thing is one of the infinite eyes of God, open upon the great dream which is the universe, observing from a unique vantage point.

God, therefore, is a great Stereo.

Daydream _____

_____

_____

_____

_____

_____

_____

_____

_____

_____

_____

_____

_____

_____

_____

_____

_____

_____

_____

_____

Tools of Creativity

A question is often asked: "Where do you get your ideas?"

The answer is: "Where *don't* you?"

The tools of creativity are all around us. In fact, *anything* can set off an idea like an enthusiastic spark. In moments ideas are jumping around you like popcorn, while you look at the world with receptive eyes.

The trick is being open and willing to see things outside their usual places—things arranged in new ways and in different, startling combinations and patterns.

The last step is to imbue them with *meaning*.

Thought _____

_____
_____
_____
_____
_____
_____
_____
_____
_____
_____
_____
_____

Escape Options

If you jump up and down and flap your hands fast enough, you *might* sprout wings and take off.

You could stick your head in the sand and hope for the best.

You could grow a hard shell, retreat inside, and "hide."

Or you can get real.

Insight _____

_____
_____
_____
_____
_____
_____
_____
_____
_____
_____
_____
_____
_____
_____
_____

The Stranger in the Rain

On the late afternoon streets, everyone hurries along, going about their own business.

Who is the person walking in front of you on the rain-drenched sidewalk?

He is covered with an umbrella, and all you can see is a dark coat and the shoes striking the puddles.

And yet, this person is the hero of his own life story.

He is the love of someone's life.

And what he can do may change the world.

Imagine *being him* for a moment.

And then continue on your own way.

Daydream _____

_____

_____

_____

_____

_____

_____

_____

_____

Hypocrites

Hypocrites are often secretly tempted to undertake journeys along the same questionable paths they are accusing others of pursuing.

With one foot on the disdained path and the other caught in a bear trap of righteousness . . . no wonder they are so angry—it hurts them twice as much.

And now that you know their plight, don't be too hard on them.

Thought _____

_____

_____

_____

_____

_____

_____

_____

_____

_____

_____

_____

_____

_____

_____

_____

The Rules of Trust

Be nice to everyone.

Be friends with a few.

Trust one person: yourself.

Sounds harsh? You bet. No rules are absolute, but it is often wisest to "pretend" this one is—at least until we learn to better *understand* the true nature of trust.

Insight _____

_____

_____

_____

_____

_____

_____

_____

_____

_____

_____

_____

_____

_____

_____

_____

_____

Wise Clichés

What's wrong with clichés?

A cliché is something that was once powerfully exciting, good, and true, but with excessive use has lost its meaning. *Your eyes are like stars* is no longer as meaningful as it was the first time around, ages ago, when some inspired lover used the phrase.

And yet, because of their original power, clichés still serve an important role. They are non-threatening comfort food for the imagination, a beloved fount of familiarity. Conjuring easily evocative images, they facilitate understanding and therefore speed up communication.

And sometimes, it is more important to be simple—to come across precisely and make basic sense—than to say something flashy, impressive (and incomprehensible) in an exciting, new way.

Don't be afraid of clichés. Common wisdom is milking a cliché for all its worth, but without annoying anyone.

If you want to be heard and understood, maintain a fine balance of clichés and new terms in your conversation.

Daydream _____

_____

_____

Speaking Terms

If you've had a fall-out with a loved one, and you aren't on speaking terms, ask yourself this:

Who decides the terms?

And then, feel free to decide otherwise.

Thought _____

_____
_____
_____
_____
_____
_____
_____
_____
_____
_____
_____
_____
_____
_____
_____
_____
_____
_____
_____
_____

The Point of Light

The star is a tiny point of light in the deep that is the night heavens. Its distant neighbors are more distant than the farthest thing on earth we know.

The star is surrounded by an infinite number of other stars in a stream of light that is the galaxy.

The galaxy is a point of light, and its closest neighbors are other galaxies in a cluster.

The galactic cluster is a point of light forming a sea of membranes and strings wound and coiled inward and outward.

The strings and membranes recede into a point of light that is but one in a shower of the sparks hitting the grate of your fireplace.

You blink.

Insight _____

_____

_____

_____

_____

_____

_____

Innocence

Innocence is often confused with simple ignorance, with naïveté or unawareness and unfamiliarity with the facts of life.

Instead, true innocence is a complex state of mind that *follows* extensive and difficult experience and yet acknowledges the *eternal* possibility of good—despite knowing the full extent of darkness present in reality.

Innocence is the secret attribute of wisdom.

Daydream _____

_____

_____

_____

_____

_____

_____

_____

_____

_____

_____

_____

_____

_____

_____

_____

_____

Fool's Vantage

A fool sees all things to be, at one point or another, finite. That is because he or she perceives but the completion of certain stages, and is incapable of observing any farther.

Well. . . . It's time to take the fool outside and up on the mountaintop!

Thought _____

_____
_____
_____
_____
_____
_____
_____
_____
_____
_____
_____
_____
_____
_____
_____
_____
_____
_____

The Violin and the Flute

The sound of a single violin playing evokes an immediate sense of emotional complexity, of rich dark layers of human history and sophisticated classical civilization.

The sound of a single flute playing recalls its opposite—the living wilderness, untamed fragile nature in its youthful simplicity.

Put them together, and observe a wondrous lace *fabric* being woven out of the air itself, as innocence and complexity are entwined as lovers in the wind. . . .

Insight _____

_____

_____

_____

_____

_____

_____

_____

_____

_____

_____

_____

_____

_____

_____

Imagine

Come now, can you really imagine not existing?

No?

Hmm, I wonder why.

Daydream _____

_____
_____
_____
_____
_____
_____
_____
_____
_____
_____
_____
_____
_____
_____
_____
_____
_____
_____
_____
_____
_____

Face

The greatest power of all is the ability to face Truth in all its aspects—external or personal—and look calmly in the Face of Shame.

Humiliation is the final test of character.

Be not afraid to lose face and you will have gained a glorious, permanent one.

Thought _____

_____

_____

_____

_____

_____

_____

_____

_____

_____

_____

_____

_____

_____

_____

_____

_____

_____

_____

October 28

Fascination

Fascination can lead us into really strange places.

Some are marvelous, some are dangerous, some are fascinating in themselves.

Fascination is one of the many faces of inspiration. It is the first glimmer of the great, shining, golden hoard just around the corner. . . .

Just be prepared to find fool's gold, most of the time.

Insight _____

_____

_____

_____

_____

_____

_____

_____

_____

_____

_____

_____

_____

_____

The One Place

There is a place in everyone's home to which we come when we feel the need to be safe and comfortable.

For some of us, it's a comfy chair. For others, the bed. Or a familiar soft spot on the sofa. Or even the bathroom.

It's a place to put up your feet, curl into a catlike bundle, and relax all your inhibitions.

Just think—of all the places to be, this is *the one place* in which you are tangibly *anchored* in the world around you, like a peg that's slipped into its uniquely shaped hole.

You feel your place. And possibly you feel your "place" in the scheme of things.

And, as you occupy it long enough, it is possible that you might come to feel your *true purpose*.

Daydream _____

_____
_____
_____
_____
_____
_____
_____

Motives and Acts

Motives do not matter only when the resulting acts are harmless.

Acts do not matter only when the motives behind them are dark.

Do not be misled.

Thought _____

_____

_____

_____

_____

_____

_____

_____

_____

_____

_____

_____

_____

_____

_____

_____

_____

_____

_____

_____

Darkness and Radiance

The autumn wind blows numbing cold, and twilight paints the evening indigo.

The orange carved pumpkin sits on the windowsill, grinning like the moon's strange cousin, and its teeth are flames.

Don't be afraid.

You carry our own heat inside you, and it is stronger than anything.

In the closing darkness, radiate the sunflower-golden warmth and put the Jack-o'-Lantern to shame. . . .

Insight _____

_____

_____

_____

_____

_____

_____

_____

_____

_____

_____

_____

_____

_____

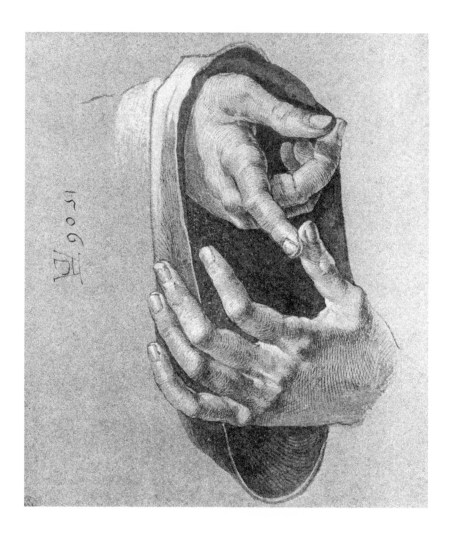

Sugar and Salt

Neither sugar nor salt tastes particularly good by itself. Each is at its best when used to season other things.

Love is the same way.

Use it to "season" people.

Daydream _____

_____

_____

_____

_____

_____

_____

_____

_____

_____

_____

_____

_____

_____

_____

_____

_____

_____

_____

_____

_____

Your Voice

A choir is made up of many voices, including yours and mine. If, one by one, all go silent, then all that will be left are the soloists.

Don't let a loud few determine the nature of the sound. It makes for poor harmony and diminishes the song.

Register.

Vote.

Thought _____

_____

_____

_____

_____

_____

_____

_____

_____

_____

_____

_____

_____

_____

_____

_____

Pleasure: A Streetlight

There is something indescribable about a streetlight against the backdrop of night, especially in winter.

Its light is cool, unlike the sun. And the bulb casts a soft glow around it, fading gently into the darkness.

If there is a snowfall, every white snowflake reflects the streetlights like a prism. And as you watch each lamp in passing, it seems, a rainbow appears in its glowing corona. . . .

There is magic here.

The streetlights are captured moons, lined up for your personal illumination.

Their encasing glass must not be broken, otherwise they will flee upward into the sky.

Insight _____

_____

_____

_____

_____

_____

_____

_____

From the Potbellied Jar

Find an ancient, potbellied jar buried in the sand. Rub its sides to clear the dust, and uncork it, to release a genie.

When the genie offers you three wishes, tell him you will think on it. Meanwhile, ask the genie about his own life in those thousands of years gone by—stories of the ancient, sunlit times, and the days of legend.

As the genie settles next to you, you listen. And the two of you sip tea and share secrets, while the years again pass by.

When your first gray hairs appear, tell the genie you no longer need three wishes granted, only one. And then, spend the remaining days of your lifetime deciding on that one wish.

In the end, you thank the genie. And with your last and only wish you set him free.

He did grant you, after all, exactly what was unasked.

Daydream _____

_____
_____
_____
_____
_____

Masquerade

A costume party is a great opportunity to be someone you secretly want to be, or to express your wild side.

It's interesting that, for many of us, our "wild side" and our "dream persona" is one and the same.

A masquerade gives an excuse for flamboyant behavior that may be otherwise embarrassing or unacceptable or too over-the-top.

Think about *what* your favorite persona and perfect costume might be—and *why*. Could it be that it's simply the most *empowered aspect* of your true self?

And now, think: do you really need to hide that wonderful, over-the-top "you" behind that mask? Especially if it enhances you as a well-rounded person?

Maybe it's okay to let at least a *glimmer* of this part of your personality come out and play openly, at other times during the year.

Thought _____

_____

_____

_____

_____

_____

Humane

The eyes of a living creature are often the most expressive features.

Look closely.

That cat is blinking—it is smiling at you.

Watch long enough and find *humanity*.

Insight _____

_____
_____
_____
_____
_____
_____
_____
_____
_____
_____
_____
_____
_____
_____
_____
_____
_____
_____

Seven Rules of Sanity

1. Don't be righteous—do what's right.

2. Don't be good—do good.

3. Don't be a martyr—survive and endure.

4. Don't be a victim—insist and establish.

5. Don't drudge for a living—create for life.

6. Don't judge others—observe them in yourself.

7. Don't be an idiot—be willing to change your opinion.

Daydream _____

_____

_____

_____

_____

_____

_____

_____

_____

_____

_____

_____

_____

November 8

Scented Window Shopping

Moving along the cozy street, the visual display is an infinite carousel.

The windows of the shops are peek-holes into other worlds, and the doorways are portals into the imagination.

As you pass by, smell the sugar perfume of the bakery, the floral aroma of the bed and bath, the musk of the clothing boutique, the subdued sterile-freshness of the jeweler, the strange old-new brew of the bookstore, and the mixed bouquet of the gift shop.

Today, let your nose do the browsing.

Thought _____

When the Other is Wrong

When you are absolutely certain the other person is wrong and you are correct . . .

- Don't rage
- Don't accuse
- Don't judge
- Don't insult
- Don't scream and cry
- Don't attempt wild feats of logic to prove your point

Instead, gently defuse the situation, and subtly change the subject. . . .

And then use all your formidable ability as a fair and sentient being to *show*, by your own example and deeds, the validity of your argument.

Be prepared to work at it for a long time. Be aware there are no guarantees. Be open, ultimately, to changing your own position.

Whatever happens, never close your eyes to the facts. It's the one sure way to remain in the light.

Insight _____

_____

_____

_____

The Fringe of Involvement

Skeptics or believers of the paranormal both come in two flavors—those who valiantly try to disprove the existence of the paranormal, and those who try to prove it.

Both kinds believe too strongly pro and con. The only ones properly qualified to investigate should be merely on the fringe of involvement.

Unfortunately, they are the ones who never bother. . . .

The moral of this observation?

Sometimes, being on the fringe of involvement is an excellent place to be.

Daydream _____

_____

_____

_____

_____

_____

_____

_____

_____

_____

_____

_____

Know Thyself

To know yourself is to know everyone else.

Yes, it really *is* that simple.

But, keep in mind, for the greater part of our lives, we really know close to nothing about ourselves.

Why?

Half our lifetime is spent "discovering" ourselves. And the other half—getting reconciled to the facts.

Try to make the second process as swift as possible.

Thought _____

_____
_____
_____
_____
_____
_____
_____
_____
_____
_____
_____
_____
_____
_____

What is Love?

"What is Love?" asked the ancient poets and the modern psychologists.

And the world spent millennia answering this question.

There are as many answers as there are living beings. And each answer is as messy and complicated as the others.

Now, a better question is, *why?*

Love is simple.

Insight _____

_____
_____
_____
_____
_____
_____
_____
_____
_____
_____
_____
_____
_____
_____

Seeing the Bully

Have you, or someone you know, ever been bullied?

Have *you* ever bullied anyone?

The answer most likely is "yes" and "yes."

We are profoundly traumatized by the former but usually don't remember, recognize, or even notice instances of the latter.

Time to get our inner vision checked.

Daydream _____

_____
_____
_____
_____
_____
_____
_____
_____
_____
_____
_____
_____
_____
_____
_____
_____

Origin Story

Origin stories have a certain visceral power. Whether it's the myth of the birth of a god or the rise of a supernatural hero, it's a story of someone coming into his or her own.

The evolution from social invisibility and weakness to confidence and strength is *the* wish fulfillment dream.

But here's the reality: the final being that we become is always larger than life. The wonder is in recognizing it. . . .

Each one of us is an origin story in the making.

Thought _____

_____
_____
_____
_____
_____
_____
_____
_____
_____
_____
_____
_____
_____

Saying Goodbye

The last rusty-orange leaves are whirling down, and the trees are graphic ghosts.

The deep autumn chill is rising.

You've just said your farewells to the one you love.

Whether you or *they* are leaving, there is a sense of desolation.

But it *is* the season. The living spark is still inside, and it is all your own.

And seasons turn.

Insight _____

_____
_____
_____
_____
_____
_____
_____
_____
_____
_____
_____
_____
_____

Golden Education

Everyone is complaining about inadequate education. We blame the teachers, the parents, and the students. We blame society and curriculums. We blame politicians and the system.

What about *knowledge* itself? Seems that knowledge hasn't *educated us* about its own worth. Knowledge seriously needs to put on makeup, hire a publicist and get a marketing plan!

If knowledge were gold, there would be a gold rush to obtain it. Well, guess what?

Knowledge *is* gold. It's also platinum and diamond, and everything else bright and glorious to the imagination. But—where's the excitement?

Amazing how many of us don't know it on a visceral, gut level (think: retail, especially during the holiday shopping season)—the level necessary to create greedy fervor and promote its desirability to the public in general. So, time to remedy this?

Incite a Knowledge Rush!

Daydream _____

_____

_____

The Weight of the World

The weight of the world is a trifle, if we all put our two fingers under it and try to lift together.

Thought _____

_____

_____

_____

_____

_____

_____

_____

_____

_____

_____

_____

_____

_____

_____

_____

_____

_____

_____

_____

_____

_____

_____

_____

Wings

What are wings, but obedient limbs?

It is the mind that initiates flight.

Insight _____

_____

_____

_____

_____

_____

_____

_____

_____

_____

_____

_____

_____

_____

_____

_____

_____

_____

_____

_____

_____

Profound Humor

It is said, humor is a peculiar, idiosyncratic, personal thing. That's why no single joke works on everyone.

To be genuinely funny, a comedian has to reach deep inside and poke at his or her own *worst* vulnerability. It's the only time the laughter rings true and not merely resembles a vicious putdown of someone else. Real laughter is *never* born of insecurity, and is *not* an outgrowth of fear. Rather, it is a *recognition of absurdity*.

We laugh at ourselves most completely and genuinely when we also believe in ourselves, and feel confident and unthreatened, so that all vulnerability is seen as an honest human trait—and as such, a source of amusement.

That's when others also recognize this malleable, personal thing we find funny. And they not only feel free but are in fact *compelled* to join in.

So, start laughing at yourself and see what happens.

Giggles, like yawns, are contagious.

Daydream _____

_____

_____

_____

_____

Regardless of Season

If you feed the birds and squirrels regardless of season, if you set out a dish for the possums and the raccoons when the weather intensifies, you are the secret master of the world.

Don't tell anyone how it works. They may only figure it out for themselves.

Thought _____

_____
_____
_____
_____
_____
_____
_____
_____
_____
_____
_____
_____
_____
_____
_____
_____
_____

Pleasure: A Blanket

Never underestimate the cozy pleasure of a whisper-soft, possibly faded, often-washed, old blanket.

When the late autumn chill creeps from the blue shadowed corners, and you are waiting for the coffee or tea to boil, use the blanket as a voluminous shawl and cuddle in the generous warmth.

Wrap yourself in gentle memories of better times, smell the rich perfume of the past in the fibers of the worn fabric. Old friends and relatives are bottled in that blanket, reaching around you in a deep, perfect embrace.

An old blanket is pure, unconditional love.

Bask in it.

Insight _____

_____

_____

_____

_____

_____

_____

_____

_____

_____

_____

Urban Unicorn

The unicorn flickers in and out of your field of vision. It is white, or possibly, steel.

Watch from the corner of your eye as it soars past the cars and the landmarks, as the streets unfold and the buildings tower.

The unicorn cannot fly.

But it moves faster than you can imagine, creating the illusion.

No one else can see it but you. And even you may not see it again, unless you feel the same moment of *perfect clarity* that allowed you to remember everything—to hum the perfect song and pronounce the unicorn's true name.

And discover yours.

Daydream _____

_____
_____
_____
_____
_____
_____
_____
_____

Remembering the Dream

When you wake up from a dream, you have only a few precious moments before the details of the dream begin to dissipate and the memory fades.

Not all dreams are significant or worth remembering.

But the ones that are . . . happen again.

So, wait for the dream to return. And never be afraid. Instead, consider it an opportunity to learn something profound and possibly wondrous about yourself.

Thought _____

Earth Mother Days

Some women seem so voluptuous in every sense, richly bountiful and fertile with generous gifts of plenty, sensual and confident in their female strength, that they are called "earth mothers."

That's how some *days* feel—when they are bountiful and fertile with the power of our imagination.

Insight _____

_____
_____
_____
_____
_____
_____
_____
_____
_____
_____
_____
_____
_____
_____
_____
_____
_____
_____
_____
_____

Thanksgiving: Meditation Puzzle

You, who are taken for granted.

You are acknowledged.

Thank you.

Daydream _____

_____

_____

_____

_____

_____

_____

_____

_____

_____

_____

_____

_____

_____

_____

_____

_____

_____

_____

_____

_____

_____

_____

The Pyramid

The pyramid shape is said to hold many secrets and amazing properties.

One of them is a sense of wonder.

Thought _____

_____

_____

_____

_____

_____

_____

_____

_____

_____

_____

_____

_____

_____

_____

_____

_____

_____

_____

_____

Winter Rose

In the depths of winter, a burgundy rose blooms on your windowsill.

On the other side of the glass the snowstorm roils. You think of the Snow Queen as you draw forward to inhale the musk of the winter rose.

Since there are no cruel, broken shards of a magic mirror in your eyes, your heart remains warm.

You smile, then draw back, nearer to the golden hearth.

Insight _____

_____
_____
_____
_____
_____
_____
_____
_____
_____
_____
_____
_____
_____
_____
_____
_____

Little Things

Life is best viewed as a series of little things.

The little things—events, impressions, emotions, insights, reactions, inspirations—fall in line, one after another, to make up your single day, your week, your month, your year, your decade. . . .

Life is a ruler stick. A ruler has notches to mark various units of measure, from tiniest to largest, and you can choose to measure according to any scale.

But the basis always comes down to the smallest units. They are the ones you truly experience and live through. All the others—days, weeks, months, years, decades—are only an illusion of aggregate memories, an abstraction of general impressions, a way of organizing life into related chunks and looking back.

See how important the little things are?

They are the only things that are *real*.

Live them earnestly. Whether bland, neutral, unbearable, or wonderful, each little thing is only a moment.

Daydream _____

_____

_____

Ice and Memory

Ice is most welcome in a cold drink on a hot day.

But in the heart of winter, you want a warming, hot mug with your favorite soothing brew to keep the chill away.

When you don't have anything warm at hand, even a memory can be a small substitute.

Remember a searing look of intimate eyes.

Receive the inner fire.

Thought _____

_____
_____
_____
_____
_____
_____
_____
_____
_____
_____
_____
_____
_____
_____
_____
_____

Elemental Feast

The Snow Queen married the Rain King.

Their children are Hail and Storm.

Behold their Feast.

Insight _____

An Opportunity

The holidays are a great opportunity to reboot your life.

Be sure to return to the routine with a hair-fine degree of deviation from your original plans.

Daydream _____

_____
_____
_____
_____
_____
_____
_____
_____
_____
_____
_____
_____
_____
_____
_____
_____
_____
_____
_____
_____
_____
_____
_____
_____

December 2

The Most Beautiful Light

The most beautiful light in the darkness of night is one that shines to illuminate your way home.

The second-most beautiful light is the backup flashlight you carry in your pocket.

Thought _____

_____
_____
_____
_____
_____
_____
_____
_____
_____
_____
_____
_____
_____
_____
_____
_____
_____
_____
_____
_____

Gift Giving

Gift giving is a true art.

1. You need to understand the person to whom you intend to give the gift.

2. You need to know what they truly want.

3. You must be able to give it to them.

Anything less is a symptom (of varying degrees, on your part) of ignorance, distance, or insult.

But if you cannot *afford* the right gift, telling the person what you *would* do if you *could*, justifies everything—as you present that not-so-perfect substitute.

Insight _____

_____

_____

_____

_____

_____

_____

_____

_____

_____

_____

_____

Winter Fireworks

Colored lights blink on and off, racing across the green boughs. Their reflections dance across exquisite glass globes and splinter into shards against tinsel thread and garlands of metallic filaments that disappear underneath the other ornaments and finery.

Shadows follow, joyful, laughing sprites.

The tree is rich with potential wonder.

All it needs is a glance from you to come *alive*.

Daydream _____

The Smile

Withhold a smile only when the smile can hurt someone.

Otherwise, let it bloom forth in a riot.

Thought _____

_____
_____
_____
_____
_____
_____
_____
_____
_____
_____
_____
_____
_____
_____
_____
_____
_____
_____
_____
_____
_____
_____
_____

Social Network Status

It's interesting how much time we spend thinking about clever things to say in our next status update on the various social networks.

What if . . . you could post your *imaginary ideal* status?

What would it be?

Insight _____

_____

_____

_____

_____

_____

_____

_____

_____

_____

_____

_____

_____

_____

_____

_____

_____

_____

_____

Perfect Justice

Justice based purely on laws is about as accurate as a portrait created out of large, low-resolution color pixels.

If you stand back far enough, it looks good.

Come any closer and the glaring approximations overtake all semblance of the original.

Justice should be viewable under the microscope, not from a telescope.

And for that it needs to be based not on law but on truth.

Daydream _____

_____

_____

_____

_____

_____

_____

_____

_____

_____

_____

_____

_____

_____

_____

_____

_____

Invisible Tuxedo

What is it about wearing a tuxedo or that little black dress, that makes us feel confident, beautiful, splendid, even invincible?

We put on formal wear and suddenly we become extraordinary.

On the days when you feel low and invisible, why not try this on for size: imagine you are wearing a fantastic tailored tuxedo or a stunning formal gown.

And then proceed with your day.

Thought _____

_____
_____
_____
_____
_____
_____
_____
_____
_____
_____
_____
_____
_____

The First Tree

The first tree grew in a forest of grass and lesser shrubs.

At first it was like all the rest. And then it kept growing, rising to tower over the other vegetation.

At some point it knew it was tall and different and strong.

The tree, new and self-aware, defined and named itself.

So must you.

Insight _____

_____
_____
_____
_____
_____
_____
_____
_____
_____
_____
_____
_____
_____
_____
_____

December 10

Warmth of the Moment

The cold stands outside and beyond, but you are wrapped in a cocoon of warmth.

It is your home. No matter if it is only a home of the moment.

Cherish it.

Daydream _____

_____
_____
_____
_____
_____
_____
_____
_____
_____
_____
_____
_____
_____
_____
_____
_____
_____
_____
_____

The Vortex

Negativity is a hungry vortex.

Negativity loves to feed on argument, disappointment, frustration, worry—all things that increase your sense of personal insignificance, and decrease your ability to *act*.

Don't get sucked in.

Counter negativity with its opposite. Feed it laughter, grins and smiles, warm reminiscences and nostalgic tales. Put it to bed with hopeful dreams.

And for dessert, serve it a song.

Thought _____

Frost the Architect

Frost grows on the window glass, forming whorl patterns of lovely, translucent geometry.

Breathe on the glass, and you give frost more ammunition.

Now it can build castles and cities and whole ice continents with your breath's vapor.

In a few blinks you can almost see the winter fairies moving in. . . .

But first, you hear the crackle of their wings.

Insight _____

_____
_____
_____
_____
_____
_____
_____
_____
_____
_____
_____
_____
_____
_____

Marriage of Elegance and Grace

What is the difference between "elegance" and "grace?" Both notions are rich with fine nuances of meaning.

Elegance suggests smooth, suave, secular style, while grace hints at spiritual, even religious finesse.

During the holidays, may your spirit be elegant and your state of grace be achieved in high style.

Daydream _____

_____
_____
_____
_____
_____
_____
_____
_____
_____
_____
_____
_____
_____
_____
_____
_____
_____
_____
_____

The Heartland

The heartland lies where the heart longs to be.

Sometimes, it takes a lifetime to find the true place to plant it.

Thought _____

_____
_____
_____
_____
_____
_____
_____
_____
_____
_____
_____
_____
_____
_____
_____
_____
_____
_____
_____
_____
_____

A Different Book

Today, take a courageous leap of the mind.

Seek out and read a completely *different* kind of book from the kind you would normally read.

Try a different genre, or a different focus. Try fiction or non-fiction. Try even a memoir, a textbook, a travelogue, a history, a wonderful "trashy" read, a political economics treatise.

Pick something that really does *not* appeal to you. Go to the section of the bookstore that you have never visited before, *ever.*

Even if being there makes you embarrassed. Even if it seems trivial, stupid, boring, *alien.* Even if it scares you.

Today, be a book berserker.

Insight _____

_____
_____
_____
_____
_____
_____
_____
_____

When Things Break

One of the most stressful feelings is when things break around you. Whether it's appliances suddenly not working properly, careful plans falling apart, or even people not being there when you need them—you feel *derailed* and out of control.

It all seems out of the blue. A new (and possibly costly) responsibility has suddenly fallen on your shoulders. Because the thing that has broken now needs to be dealt with—on top of all your other regular obligations.

What to do?

Treat this as a new starting point for all the things you have to do. And knowing this, do the best you can.

Because—even though the overall menu has changed in the middle of dinner, ultimately *you* control your entrée choices.

After all, *you* are not broken.

Daydream _____

_____

_____

_____

_____

_____

Annoying Optimist

People who are too optimistic seem annoying. This is an unfortunate misinterpretation of what an *optimist* really is.

An optimist is neither naïve, nor blind to the facts, nor in denial of grim reality. An optimist believes in the *optimal* usage of all options available, no matter how limited. As such, an optimist always sees the big picture. How else to keep track of all that's out there? An optimist is simply a proactive realist.

An idealist focuses only on the best aspects of all things (sometimes in detriment to reality); an optimist strives to find an effective solution. A pessimist sees limited or no choices in dark times; an optimist *makes* choices.

When bobbing for apples, an idealist endlessly reaches for the best apple, a pessimist settles for the first one within reach, while an optimist drains the barrel, fishes out all the apples and makes pie.

Annoying? Yes. But, oh-so tasty!

Thought _____

_____

_____

_____

_____

_____

Meditation

Meditation is a mysterious method of self-restoration.

It involves "shutting" out the outside world and, by that means, sensing the universal "presence" which is, incidentally, absolute, perfect peace.

It is basically an existential "time-out"—a way to "come up for a breath of air" out of the noisy clutter of the world.

But don't be afraid, there is nothing arcane or supernatural or creepy about the notion of taking a time-out. Ball players do it. Kids do it, when prompted by their parents. Heck, even your computer does it (and sometimes not when you want it to).

So, why not you?

A meditation can be as simple as taking a series of easy breaths, and slowly, gently counting to ten in your mind.

Insight _____

_____

_____

_____

_____

_____

_____

Pleasure: Holiday Lights

They are everywhere.

As the cold deepens and the seasonal darkness draws longer, the lights come. . . .

White winter fireflies race in necklaces around tree branches and garlanding roofs. Golden, stately flames bloom in the candles of the menorah. Rainbow bulbs wink in the green thickets of the Christmas tree. Blazing orange light consumes the Yule log.

On the streets, ghosts of Victorian nostalgia fill the storefront displays with delightful memories of things that never really *were,* except in faded picture postcards. They call to you with their scents of nutmeg and marzipan and the promise of sugarplum fairy dreams and, just past midnight, the arrival of the Nutcracker beloved of your dreams.

And all of it—holiday spirit, ethereal hopes, bittersweet memories, nostalgia, desire—is illuminated with light.

Daydream _____

_____

_____

_____

_____

_____

A Reindeer Tale

Once upon a time, the Reindeer took a running leap and jumped over the Northern Lights.

But he jumped too low, and the long fur of his beautiful, flowing tail got singed by the rainbow fires of the aurora.

To this day, the reindeer has no tail to speak of. But he is too busy pulling the Important Sleigh to notice what is lost. And he certainly doesn't complain.

What's your excuse?

Thought _____

_____

_____

_____

_____

_____

_____

_____

_____

_____

_____

_____

_____

_____

_____

_____

The Wisest King

One true king knew when to step aside and give up the reins of power—to remove his crown and relinquish his kingdom—all for the sake of glimpsing, just once in a lifetime, the face of a holy child.

He was the Fourth to follow the Star.

His gift was a secret.

The rest of his journey is unknown.

Insight _____

_____
_____
_____
_____
_____
_____
_____
_____
_____
_____
_____
_____
_____
_____
_____
_____
_____
_____

The Nutcracker

The nutcracker sits under the holiday tree, a guardian of childhood stories.

Feed him walnuts, and he will crack open a tale. . . .

Daydream _____

_____

_____

_____

_____

_____

_____

_____

_____

_____

_____

_____

_____

_____

_____

_____

_____

_____

_____

_____

_____

The Hat of Inspiration

When you need a bit of inspiration, put on a hat.

And now, imagine what it would be like to wear this hat every day. Imagine how the hat might change you, if you *had* to wear it always and could never take it off.

Now, take off the hat.

Aren't you glad you *can?*

Thought _____

_____

_____

_____

_____

_____

_____

_____

_____

_____

_____

_____

_____

_____

_____

_____

Golden Reverie

Snowflakes swirl down gently in the deep blue haze beyond the window. The outside world is a dream.

Inside, the fireplace is brightly lit, and the Yule log crackles with orange and crimson sparks.

There's a steaming mug in your hands, warming your fingers.

There's a friend seated across from you in the cozy chair, warming your heart.

There is mystery unfolding.

Insight _____

_____

_____

_____

_____

_____

_____

_____

_____

_____

_____

_____

_____

_____

Bottled Holiday Warmth

Many of us get depressed during the holidays. We tend to look around at the seething overflow of cheer everywhere—in the media, on the streets, within every social circumstance. If we are not personally caught up in the whirlwind joy, we feel inadequate, and the blue feeling intensifies and spirals.

Eventually we are like spots of gloom compared to the rest of the bubbling Happyland, when in fact we are merely the same—exactly how we have been moments before someone decided to call in the holidays.

All of this might take place not because we are all Humbug Scrooges, but because any forced mood change somehow feels artificial, unreal, and most of us are able to tell.

Indeed, festive mood is like a bottled, giddy perfume, and it gets liberally sprayed on the world around the early fall, so that all the focus tends to slip toward green fir tree boughs, red gift wrap, golden, blurry lights, and various camera angles upon a laden feast-table centerpiece. The festive fragrance also calls up people dressed in bright sweaters, smiling excessively and hugging each other, raising sparkling glasses to toast something intangible.

Sometimes, this perfume works on us, and we are caught up in the glow (in which case, ignore the rest of this entry, go, shoo!).

Other times, we are not quite in synch with it. So we wave off the overbearing scent in annoyance, not to mention, a minor allergic reaction. This is when the dissonance starts to grate, to exacerbate our irritation and our already *different* personal state. Or else, it increases the nostalgic longing for the illusory joy that seems out of reach.

Think—how unfair it is to ask anyone to rejoice when they are breaking inside, for so many reasons.

And yet . . .

And yet, the Spirit of the Holidays has a strange, healing power if we allow it to affect us. For it is the collective spirit of joy of humanity with all its rich, time-brewed traditions and rituals and primeval wonder—how can it not move us?

However, as with any proper application of scent, too much all at once is a mistake. Mood perfume must be so subtle that it enters you and me without notice, gradually, and starts to seduce with its inevitability.

One breath at a time.

Transforming us.

Then the warmth becomes real, the candles shine with a sacred light, the green boughs beckon, and the smiles touch the heart. Even if just for a moment, it is all genuine, all applicable to us, members of the human species.

It is only then that, drenched in the perfumed sweetness of verisimilitude, we can truly celebrate.

Daydream _____

_____
_____
_____
_____
_____
_____
_____
_____
_____
_____
_____
_____
_____
_____
_____
_____
_____
_____
_____
_____
_____
_____
_____
_____
_____
_____
_____
_____
_____

The Invention

A very long time ago, when the world was plain, a brilliant scientist invented a wonderful, mysterious device. When touched, it inspired you.

People from everywhere came to touch the device—and were inspired to create problems, solve all masterpieces, heal the hungry, and feed the sick. Others were inspired to invent even more amazing inventions. Soon, the world filled with technological wonders.

Because so many people touched it, the device eventually wore down and stopped working. And when the oceans rose to swallow land and rearrange the continents, everything that was left of the inspired civilization sank to the bottom.

But the memory of inspiration remains to this day. It's why so many of us unconsciously reach out to touch the things of the world, and why we reach out for each other.

There's something to be invented.

Thought _____

_____

_____

_____

_____

_____

_____

Gingerbread Room

The Gingerbread House has four walls, a roof, a door, a window, and a chimney. It is decorated with many sweet culinary delights on the outside.

But on the inside there is nothing—only the bare gingerbread walls.

It is not a real house—not until you decide to add a Gingerbread Room.

That's when the stories can move in.

They will stay in residence for as long as you abstain from taking the first gingerbread bite.

Insight _____
_____
_____
_____
_____
_____
_____
_____
_____
_____
_____
_____
_____

The Compass Rose

The compass rose is nothing but a star with an infinite number of rays pointing in all directions.

It is the one true and perfect symbol of the universe.

And it is the one most accurate symbol of *you*.

Spread your arms in an embrace, throw your head back, and prepare to receive and send coordinates of *being*. For, at last you *know*—you are the navigator, the captain, and the ship.

Daydream _____

_____

_____

_____

_____

_____

_____

_____

_____

_____

_____

_____

_____

The Future

Would you like to know your future?

If your answer is yes, think again. Not knowing is the greatest life motivator.

So enjoy, endure, survive each moment as it comes in its proper sequence—a surprise.

Thought _____

_____

_____

_____

_____

_____

_____

_____

_____

_____

_____

_____

_____

_____

_____

_____

_____

_____

The Bell

The great miraculous bell of translucent ice is suspended in mid-air.

It rings to announce endings and beginnings. And it rings because there is fresh promise and wonder in the skies.

Its clear tones resound in the placid silence of the winter day, and echo long into the silver-blue serenity of night.

The bell can only be seen at the turning of the year, when the days wind down into nothing and get ready to march out again.

When you hear the bell, you feel a tug at your heart.

It is your immortal inspiration.

Insight _____

_____
_____
_____
_____
_____
_____
_____
_____
_____

New Beginnings

The New Year is a reusable blank slate. No reservations or regrets. Every moment you can begin anew with passion.

Use the bouquet of moments well.

Daydream _____

_____
_____
_____
_____
_____
_____
_____
_____
_____
_____
_____
_____
_____
_____
_____
_____
_____
_____
_____
_____
_____

List of Illustrations

"Study Of Drapery" by Albrecht Durer, 1521.

"When In The Chronicle Of Wasted Time I See Description Of The Fairest Wights, And Beauty Making Beautiful Old Rhyme In Praise Of Ladies Dead And Lovely Knights' Shakespeare" [frame detail] by Robert Anning Bell, 1907.

"Wat Tha Thanon" photo by Tevaprapas Makklay 2009.

"Folio 27r, *The Lindisfarne Gospels*, Incipit to the Gospel of Matthew," c. 698.

"Egret, Moon and Wave," by Sesson Shûkei, 16th century Japan.

"Book of Kells, Folio 130, Incipit to Mark. *Initium evangelii.*"

"Dancing Moghul women," Auguste Racinet's *Le Costume Historique*, 1876-1888.

"Amanohasidatezu" by Japanese Painter Sesshyu.

"Wat Tha Thanon" public domain photo by Anonymous.

"Eleven-faced Kannon (ekadaza mukha)," [detail] Domyoji Temple, 9th century, photo by Ogawa Seiyou, 1930.

"Head of Eleven-faced Kannon Hokkeji" photo by Matsuoka Koumu, 1930.

"Two Gibbons Reaching for the Moon" by Ito Jakuchu, c. 1770.

"Mother Goose: The Cow Jumped Over the Moon" by Arthur Rackham.

"Pages Of Marginal Drawings For Emperor Maximilian's Prayer Book" by Albrecht Durer, 1515.

"Apollo With The Solar Disc And Diana Trying To Shield Herself From The Rays With Her Uplifted Hand" by Albrecht Durer (1471-1528).

"The So-Called Great Piece Of Turf" by Albrecht Durer, 1503.

"Mother Goose: The Fair Maid who the first of Spring" by Arthur Rackham.

"Peasant girls using chicken for divination," Russian lubok, XIXth century.

"September" by Jean Limbourg, 1400.

"Boy's Hands" by Albrecht Durer, 1506.

"Winged Man, In Idealistic Clothing, Playing a Lute" by Albrecht Durer, 1497.

ABOUT THE BOOK AND AUTHOR

The Perpetual Calendar of Inspiration
Old Wisdom for a New World

Most of the 366 daily inspirations and thoughts collected here were originally written and posted online in blog entry form on the Inspired.Us Blog, written by author and award-winning artist **Vera Nazarian**. The blog is currently live at **www.InspiredUs.com** and you are invited to visit anytime, for a new dose of inspiration.

Vera Nazarian is a two-time Nebula Award® Finalist and a 2018 Dragon Award Finalist. She immigrated to the USA from the former USSR as a kid, sold her first story at 17, and has been published in numerous anthologies and magazines, and translated into eight languages.

Her work includes *Dreams of the Compass Rose* (2002), *Lords of Rainbow* (2003), *The Clock King and the Queen of the Hourglass* (2005), collection *Salt of the Air* containing the 2007 Nebula Award-nominated "The Story of Love," 2008 Nebula Finalist novella *The Duke in His Castle,* collection *After the Sundial* (2010), *The Perpetual Calendar of Inspiration* (2010), three Jane Austen parodies, *Mansfield Park and Mummies* (2009), *Northanger Abbey and Angels and Dragons* (2010), and *Pride and Platypus: Mr. Darcy's Dreadful Secret* (2012), *Vampires are from Venus, Werewolves are from Mars: A Comprehensive Guide to Attracting Supernatural Love* (2012), *Cobweb Bride Trilogy* (2013), and the four books in the bestselling international cross-genre series **The Atlantis Grail**, now optioned for development as a feature film and/or TV series, *Qualify* (2014), *Compete* (2015), *Win* (2017), and *Survive* (2020).

After many years in Los Angeles, Vera now lives in a small town in Vermont. She uses her Armenian sense of humor and her Russian sense of suffering to bake conflicted pirozhki and make art.

In addition to being a writer, philosopher, and award-winning artist, she is also the publisher of Norilana Books.

Official website: veranazarian.com